Spiritual Living in a Sexual World

A book for Men, and their Wives who love them

By Scott R. Kraniak

1stBooks – rev. 4/4/01

This book is dedicated to My Beloved

Julie
The most understanding wife in the world!

TABLE of CONTENTS

Acknowledgments

Scriptural Consultant   Pastor Arthur Sceviour, Th.M.

Creative Consultant   Mrs. Brenda Baker
Manuscript Editor   Mrs. Brenda Baker

All Scripture References   Authorized King James Version Bible
Webster's New World Dictionary, Version 1.0, Copyright 1997
The Compact Bible Dictionary, Copyright 1967 By Zondervan Publishing House
The Bible Promise Book, By Barbour Publishing, Inc. ISBN 0-916441-87-3

Any names of places referred to in this book are real, but all names and places and references to people have been changed to protect the right to privacy of all.

I would like to give a special thanks to Brenda Baker for her encouragement and time throughout this long, long project. (It's done). Praise God!

I would also like to thank my mother and father for their constant encouragement and faith in me when I had no faith at all. Your love is indescribable!

Most of all, I would like to thank my Lord Jesus Christ for the abundant grace, love, and patience that He has shown toward me, that I still can't comprehend!

The Sun does shine after the storm.

Forward
by

Dr. Walter Croom , General Director
Military Evangelism, Inc.
Aberdeen, Maryland

Walt Croom is the Author of *Overcoming Fear ,Winning Over Depression* and *Beginning a Counseling Center*
He has a Ph.D. in religious counseling and is founder of a counseling center.

Wise old king Solomon wrote, "Let thine eyes look right on, and let thine eyelids look straight before thee." (Proverbs 4:25) Obviously Solomon knew much about youthful temptation and offered a remedy against it.

It's a problem for believers to stay focused because every believer has the world the flesh and the devil to contend with. John reminds us in his epistle to be on guard against the lust of the flesh, the lust of the eyes and the pride of life. (I John 2:16)

Satan, who is our arch enemy, does everything in his power to change the believers focus. Since Satan knows our weaknesses he goes about setting traps for the believer. He knows there are certain things he can dangle before a believer to get him off cue- to change focus.

Satan knows that some men have a strong desire for worldly possessions while others desire power. Others have an insatiable desire to fulfill their sexual fantasies with the opposite sex.

In his book, Spiritual Living in a Sexual World, Scott Kraniak deals with the lust of the flesh- "girl watching".

The lust of the flesh- "girl watching" is extremely common among those who do not know Christ. When an attractive young women walks into their sphere they pause to consider this lovely specimen of humanity. But for many, especially those outside of Christ, it goes beyond admiring their beauty to lusting after their body. Christians, while more reserved, are also tempted to look and fulfill some unbiblical sexual fantasy.

People who make girl watching a habit usually have more going on in their minds than just honest appreciation of God's handwork.

The Author of this book, "Spiritual Living in a Sexual World" was not always focused on the things of Christ. For many years he was not a believer and therefore did not make any attempt to conform his life to the teaching of Scripture. Consequently he developed habits of thinking and behavior that would eventually enslave him.

For Him, his escape into sexual fantasies began by innocently looking at his dad's pornographic magazines. One day something wonderful happened in His life. He became a believer in Jesus Christ. Almost immediately he became convicted about his fondness for girl watching and sexual fantasies. the Scripture's began to make it abundantly clear that God calls believers to a life of purity and holiness before the Lord.

Over a period of time it became evident to him that he could never grow as a believer until he broke these old thinking and behavior patterns. He had to say no to his old ways and yes to Christ. But how could he do this? How can one break ingrained habits? It had become evident to him that he had become ensnared, trapped.

It also became evident to him that he lacked the power to break this habit of lusting and fantasizing on his own. In his search for truth he turned to the scripture and found the much desired relief and help for which he was longing.

I would recommend this book to anyone who is old enough to digest its content. Clear thinking is important in these difficult times, focused living is imperative.

In his book the Author also shares suggestions to the father who is trying to keep his children pure in this age of sexual perverseness. You will also find wise instruction for the young woman and how she can be an encouragement to her husband who is struggling with girl watching and impure thoughts.

Scott Kraniak will bring you back to the Scripture where clear thinking and focused living can be accomplished.

Walt Croom Ph.D.

INTRODUCTION

(the spirit is willing but the flesh is weak) ***II Corinthians 1:3-4***

One of the things that I wish I could change most in my life is that I would have accepted the Lord Jesus as my Personal God and Savior sooner, maybe when I was still a child or even a teenager. I always wonder what it would have been like to be a young Christian male going through school, adolescence, dating, and on to early adulthood. Well, I can't change that; but I can use what I've learned to help others and to bring glory to the Lord. The Bible says that all things work together for the good to those who love the Lord. I believe this whole heartily and feel this book is a result of it.

Since I was not saved until later in my life, I experienced firsthand just how evil, wicked, and tempting the things of the world can be. I know, firsthand, the sins that so easily control us and how Satan can convince us that it's all OK. For different people the sins that control us can be as varied as we are different; but for me it was the "sins of the flesh". If you mention this to the world they just don't get it. To the world this type of behavior is considered normal and just as "American" as apple pie, hot dogs, and baseball. The Bible calls it lust, the world calls it "girl watching". No matter what you call it, it's wrong! To most people, on the surface it appears to be so harmless that they dismiss it all with sentiments like "boys will be boys" and "you're not a man if you don't". The odds of finding support to condemn it are slim. Never-the-less, the approval of the world is not my aim. The Bible tells us clearly, over and over again, that it is sin. Unfortunately, "knowing" that something is wrong is not always enough to prevent us humans from actually doing it.

In this book I deal with a specific problem. My focus is on the Christian man (young, old, married or single) and specifically those of us who have an extreme weakness of the flesh—those of us who just can't stop looking, whether on the beach or on the job. In dealing with this subject I'll take you from boyhood to married life, I'll point out the dangers and the myths, and most importantly I'll show you, through the Word of God and through my own personal experiences, just how devastating this "seemingly" innocent habit can be. I've also devoted a chapter in this book to the wives of men with this tendency toward the flesh—how wives can help and also how they can hurt the situation.

From you single men, caught in the struggle with unrelenting temptation, to you Dads who are raising boys, to you teenagers, and to you wives, I think you will all find this book both enlightening and even humorous at times. And this being a Christian-based book, I've tried as hard as possible to keep it proper, chaste, and tasteful in a way that does not take from the sometimes sensitive worldly material that has to be dealt with. My aim is to comfort those with the comfort that I was comforted with;(Matthew 26:41), and to bring the Christian male into a deeper, purer, and more victorious walk with the Lord. Even though in this present age the odds "seem" to be stacked against us, we "know" that we are "more than conquerors" through the power and might of our Lord and Savior Jesus Christ!

In Christ

Scott R. Kraniak

CHAPTER 1

A monster in the making

Matthew 26:41

One of the biggest mistakes a man can make is to believe this lie, "It's OK to look once, it's the second look that is sin and brings a man to lust." This couldn't be further from the truth.

Studies estimate that about one in 12 Americans has a sex addiction, and that 65 percent of those are professionals with college degrees. "It's not just for dirty old men anymore".

In my conversion experience there have been many things to overcome, but none has been so difficult as breaking the bondage of the lust of the flesh. I've been saved for over seventeen years now and throughout this time I've experienced many struggles over sin. As I look back at my victories and failures, the greatest struggle of all had to be the lust of the flesh. And though the strong hold is past, not unlike alcoholism, it's just one "look" away. For a man with this weakness, living in today's world makes it ten times more difficult. When I first tried to kick the habit, I learned an important lesson from the Lord, you can't stop or do anything apart from Him. Anything done, whether good or bad, if done apart from God, is destined to fail. I remember trying to stop smoking and the torment it put me through. I was about a two-pack-a-day guy. I could not put a cigarette down until it was finished. After I ate, I had to smoke. When I got up in the morning, I had to smoke. You name it and I had to smoke after it, during it, or before it. So attempting to overcome this was no easy feat. I tried the gum and the always-a-failure taper method, but all to no avail. The girl I was dating at the time was also a smoker, but not as heavy as I. When she stopped, I knew I had to stop also, but how? I desired not just the nicotine but the whole attitude of smoking. I loved opening a fresh pack and the smell it produced, the packing down of a fresh pack and the lighting up of the first smoke. When I had to think or when I was nervous there was nothing like it! To this day, I can't deny that I still consider it one of the most enjoyable things to do. But the fact is, I don't smoke anymore, and I haven't in over fourteen years. Yet to my amazement, every now and then, I still get a craving. "Amazing!"

The smoking itself was not the only draw to smoking. I also enjoyed the people who would smoke, and the places where I went to smoke. I even felt that "cool" feeling that first got me hooked back in high school. It was all part of the strong hold. It took time to develop these thought responses. It wasn't overnight that I became a "smoker" and it would take just as much reprogramming and major prayer to stop. There are many things in our lives that, in time, can control

1

us, and if we are not careful, they can overtake us. So what does this have to do with girl watching? Well, it's a lot like an addiction, whether it is smoking or gambling or whatever starts to overpower you. In my experience as a Christian I was able, through God, to overcome my drinking and drugs with ease. My foul language was just removed. With some people these areas might have been, or still are, strong holds. We are all different. But in my case, *"Girl Watching"* was my burden to bear. Like any addiction, and I do consider it an addiction, it took time to develop into an overpowering monster. It wasn't just one look, it was years of letting in the filth and evils of the world. I remember when I was eight or nine being taken to, what I would consider, an R-rated movie with my parents, figuring I was too young to understand. Now, my parents were a good all American mom and dad. It was just the era of the free-sex sixties and early seventies. Sex was never demonized as it should have been, but it was often glamorized. There were always pornographic materials in the home. I knew where all the dirty magazines were hidden in my parent's bedroom, and the bathroom always had some reading paraphernalia at arms reach. When the early teens hit, all my guy friends could be found huddled around an old home movie projector, watching these old black and white, no-sound, skin flicks. One friend of mine gathered a massive collection of dirty magazines from his dad. We would all hide them in our secret meeting hide out. They were like gold! We would devour each page almost to the point of drooling. In situations like this, it doesn't take long for sin to overwhelm. And if left unchecked, sins like masturbation, sexual perversion and experimentation can often follow, plus, add the boiling hormones of a teenage boy, and you have a recipe for disaster. Most of all, I feel the overexposure to pornography was a major contributor to the rapid and descending corruption of my thought patterns and sexual evaluation of all girls and then onto women. In some cases, this can carry over to the wife and often leads to sexual and emotional problems there. It was a combination of the times, society, and a lack of a relationship with God. If you do not know it's wrong, if your dad is into it, and Satan is surely all for it, it's only a matter of time before you're past the point of no return. For an example, I was speaking to someone about the problems of violence today against women. I was given an education on all the latest support groups and government programs that deal with these issues. All the material was for the after-the-fact rehabilitation, which is all great. The problem is, no one is dealing with, or even knows, the cause. It's really simple, at least for a believer, no accountability to any higher authority, no dad to go to for true wisdom, and most of all, a society that glorifies Rape, Sex, Violence and depicts all women as sex objects and all men as cold, ruthless, sex starved animals. And if you go with the evolution conspiracy, then we are all just animals anyway, there is no creator, we are all just a big cosmic accident. Then why not just go with your own selfish desires. You know the slogan; "Just do it?" Well, everybody is!

2

In my case, and I think for a lot of men, the pornography to which we were exposed always depicted women being raped, tied up, domineering, and of course they were always the most beautiful women to walk the earth. Combine that with the churning and sometimes overwhelming hormones of a teenage boy, and you have one dangerous developing mind. Now I'm not one of the people spreading the "blame my parent and society escape." What I do blame is an old sin nature, a fallen world, and a master deceiver. That was a long time ago. Today, in the late nineties, with MTV, the Internet, and a complete breakdown in our families, I shudder to think what the men of the late twenty-first century will be like. What kind of fathers will they be and what kind of leaders will they become? Watching a pretty lady walk by might seem harmless, but there is much more to it. What do you think about? How often do you think about it? What do you do about it? Yes, I know the damage is done and it seems too overbearing, but you can have victory! You must have victory! For you single men, your testimony, your sanctification, and your future family will all be affected by what you do and don't do now. For the husbands and fathers, your relationship and union with your wife, both emotionally and physically, and with your children as their spiritual leader, will all be placed in jeopardy. Now is the time to make a change! Not alone, for it is impossible but with the Lord's mighty hand. I know that to the world it might not seem important or of any significance, but let me say this, by this one perversion, this one attitude, this total unaccountability rests the entire spiritual future of this nation and, in time, this world. We must realize that Satan knows where to attack. He knows the divine institutions that God has established to stabilize this world and maintain harmony, even among the unsaved. Be it the divine institution of volition or nations or marriage or family, he knows that by destroying one, the others won't be far behind. It's amazing to me that the world does not see this importance. They search and look to so many worldly wisdoms, but never see the obvious. Destroy the marriage, then you destroy the family. Destroy the family and you destroy the nation. It's as simple as one plus one equals two. Is it happening today? Take a look around you. What's the biggest, most obvious seller and motivator that's on all of our minds. Is it not sex? And why is it sex? Why did Satan choose that particular sin? Well, when we read proverbs ***Proverbs 6:25*** *Lust not after her beauty in thine heart; neither let her take thee with her eyelids.****Proverbs 6:26*** *For by means of a whorish woman a man is brought to a piece of bread: and the adulteress will hunt for the precious life.* ***Proverbs 6:27*** *Can a man take fire in his bosom, and his clothes not be burned?* and many other portions of scripture, we find one particular point driven home to men; men you have a weakness, you have an area in your flesh which is liken unto an open wound; tender, if you will, an area that leaves you vulnerable and without rationality, that is sex and the seductions of a woman. Now before I continue, let me go into this in some detail because I know it can be a tender spot for some women. Why does the Bible seem to portray

3

women as this sexual, destructive creature bent on bringing down every man she encounters, and then portraying men as helpless victims just trying to live a spiritual life? The answer is clear and precise. First, the Bible does not depict all women that way, and if you read those verses in context, you'll find that the focus is not on the women but on the men and their weakness. It's simply stating this fact, that men, you have a weakness. To avoid succumbing and falling into sin, avoid these types of situations and people, because you will fall! Do not think that you can resist the temptation, you can't. The Bible is stating a fact that in this fallen world there are fallen people there's no denying it, *2Co 11:14 And no marvel; for Satan himself is transformed into an angel of light. 2Co 11:15 Therefore it is no great thing if his ministers also be transformed as the ministers of righteousness; whose end shall be according to their work* And yes, there are some women, not all, that do use their sexuality to get what they want. Men, stay away from this kind! Does not the Bible speak much about the other kind, the virtuous, sanctified women of God? Most women do not have this problem to the degree that men do. If it were so, then God would have warned them also. God made us and knows that men are seduced by a look, women are by word and romance. It's a long term exposure for women that brings them down. So what does all this mean to Satan? He knows that to bring down all, he must bring down men. Hence comes the sexual element, sex on TV, sex in the movies, sex on commercials, sex in magazines and sex on the internet. No matter where you look, sex can be found. Is it working? The answer is plain to see. The first wave has already struck and the damage is done. How? Well by destroying the father figure in the home, simply, he's so distracted by sex, that having it overcomes all else in motivation. First, he gets a girl pregnant. In most cases he doesn't stick around, which leaves a child without a father (some think that's just fine and children can get along just fine without a dad). You know that can't be true because it's not part of God's plan, *Eph 5:31 For this cause shall a man leave his father and mother, and shall be joined unto his wife, and they two shall be one flesh..* Now you have a child without a dad, and a wife without a husband. The destruction has begun! And don't tell me some social government or a support group can fix it. With this damage done the family is gone, and the nation will follow. Remember, someday these young children will be moms and dads, husbands and wives. They will be leaders, maybe even the president. What will they have to fall back on? From whence will their wisdom come, their value of what's right and wrong? God help us all, for it is already in its second stages. Maybe we can't save the world, maybe we can't change our nation, but what we can change is ourselves by taking the first step of giving ourselves and our families over to the Lord. Judgment begins at the house of God. Let's be about our Father's business.

CHAPTER 2

Just looking

Proverbs 6:25

One of the things that I've learned in my years of being a Christian is that there is no room for curiosity. When the Bible speaks of wisdom as being important, it was not for nothing. Godly wisdom is something more than just "knowing" the Word of God—it's living, breathing and committing your very existence to the Word of God. Godly wisdom is knowing what God would do in this situation. I like that new slogan that's going around that asks the question "What would Jesus do?" It sounds so simple, yet so true. If there is one principle that I would love to be able to always live by it would be that one. In every situation just ask the question "What would Jesus do?" You know I've heard the old bit about hanging out at bars to reach the unsaved for Christ and I've heard Christian men say "When I'm looking at a woman passing by I'm just admiring God's handiwork". Brother let me tell you it's just plain dangerous! You might say, "Oh I can handle myself, I know when I'm in over my head". That usually means it's already too late. If you're going to live by God's Word then you have to stop and ask yourself right now, "Do I believe that all of God's Word is true or just parts of it? Do I take each and every word serious or just pick and choose only what I want to hear." The Bible says in Matt 5:27,28 when we lust after a woman we have committed adultery in the eyes of God. "It can't be" you might say, but what God has said is exactly what God means! Believe me, I've been there, I've tried to look at it a hundred different ways and it still reads the same: Yes, to look at a woman, then to lust after her is the same thing as going out to a bar, meeting a girl, taking her home, and having intercourse with her. Well, you might say "I'm just looking, I'm not lusting". Let me give you an example, let's say you're walking down the beach with your wife and a beautiful woman in a G-string walks by. Now stop, replace that picture of that woman with an old grungy fishermen. Now you still might glance over out of curiosity, but most likely you wouldn't give him a second look other than to make sure you don't walk into him. Now again, put back the scantily clad woman. When your eyes first notice her, what's the first thing you think and/or do? Do you say "I better move a little to the left so I don't run into this person"; or do you maybe just glance over and pass her by as just one of the many bits of sea shore you've been admiring? Brother my guess, if you're like any other guy, this is what happens. You're looking around, your eyes spot her and immediately your eyes lock onto first her chest, then her legs, and maybe even her face. And if you're alone you might even try to make eye contact just for the heck of it. I know you're probably feeling "At least I didn't turn around to see her from the rear". Listen, no matter how you look at it, it's all sexual. It's all lust. The next thought after looking is "touching". You've just cheated on your wife, you've sinned against God. Looking is lusting! Stopping seems impossible, I know. It's like training yourself not to yell "ouch" when you step on a nail. And the longer you were exposed to pornography before your conversion to Christ, the harder it's going to be to stop. The more years of hanging out with the guys, the more difficult it's going to be to say "No". Most of all, the more you like it the worse are your chances of ever gaining victory. But please, don't get discouraged. There is hope and there is a way! Remember you are not alone in this struggle for sexual purity—God Himself is with you. For that matter, don't even "think" you can do it yourself. Besides our own old sin nature and our past programming, we have even a bigger foe: the prince of the air, the master deceiver, yes, Satan himself. He knows your weak point whether it be eating too much or lying or whatever. He'll be on you from the very first day that you try to stop. The funny thing is, for myself, I never thought I had a problem with lust and pornography until I got saved. You see, Satan doesn't bother with the unsaved because he is content with the fact that they are already his. Before you got saved he didn't care what you did, whether it was good or bad. As long as you were not a child of God you were automatically a child of the devil, *John 8:44 Ye are of your father the devil, and the lusts of your father ye will do.* Satan didn't care if you spent every waking moment in a porn shop or even if you were a volunteer for the Red Cross. You were his, but now that you are saved you are not his and he's mad. If he can't have you, then he either wants to kill you (which he can't possibly do unless God allows) or he wants to destroy your testimony and leave you an unfruitful Christian living in defeat. However, we are more than conquerors,*Romans 8:37 Nay, in all these things we are more than conquerors through him that loved us.*

The first step in overcoming any obstacle is to admit that there is one. Do you believe that "just looking" is sin? Do you think you have a problem with lust and/or pornography? Do you feel it's wrong? Is it destroying your walk with the Lord and your spiritual growth? I know that if you're reading this book then you have realized that there is a problem and you've taken that most important step. God bless you brother! Sometimes the world and Satan himself have a way of letting us think that we can touch without getting burned. And if you play the world's game long enough you might even fool yourself into thinking that you're not getting burned: "I can look, I can peak a little, what's the big deal". My friend, the Bible has very definitive language when in comes to "just looking". The Bible speaks often of the "body" of Christ; sometimes its speaking of "the church" itself, sometimes it's speaking of the literal body of Jesus. When it's referring to "the church", we see God describing it as a literal body and how the function of one part can have lasting effects on the others—can the hands exist

6

without the head, or the toes without the feet, and if one part is corrupted the whole body can suffer loss. So how can this corruption manifest itself? Well it can take on many forms, but the most prevalent way that corruption enters is what I call the letting in through the "eye gate". We have two primary ways of letting in evil. One is by hearing: the "ear gate". And the other is by seeing: the "eye gate". Through these two means the whole body can take on corruption. You see, our minds our somewhat like video recorders. We are constantly recording billions of images throughout our life and storing them up in our memory banks. The interesting thing is how our minds filter, screen, and categorize these images and thoughts to be pulled up at a later time when the proper stimuli is introduced. Sometimes these images will be recalled for no apparent reason at all, and to our own amazement, memories are replayed in our mind that we never even knew were there. For an example, I often recall an amazing image of my own that baffles me with its purpose. I have this image of myself holding my uncle's hand as we walk down the streets of Brooklyn and then going into a soda shop to purchase an ice cream cone. This image is as clear as day, and only after relaying it to my mother did I find out that I was three years old. How she knew this was that day was the day that my great grandmother died and my uncle took me out during the wake, keeping me busy while my family paid their respect. "Big deal", you might say and maybe so; but the fact that's intriguing is that I was only three years old. I have no recollection of anything else in my life until much later. You see, what we take in is there in our minds forever. No matter if we acknowledge it or not, it's there. There's no erase button on the human mind. This can be good and bad. Obviously it's not good in the case of those bad thoughts and pictures that we collect. You see, once you look at that girl in the bathing suit, she's in there for life. If you try—which I don't advise you to do—you can probably recall every naked woman, every sexual encounter, every pornographic piece of material that you ever were exposed to. How did you, in the first place, develop fantasies with naked women without first seeing one? In this case, the question of "what came first, the chicken or the egg", the answer is simple: the chicken. So what do you do with all these sinful images? Well unfortunately they are there for ever; but what we can do is not add to the collection. You see, if our mind desires to fantasize it needs a thought or even a picture to induce it. How far back our mind has to dig and search will determine how difficult our war against the flesh will be. If you just lusted after a woman at the local supermarket or just read the latest issue of some girlie magazine it won't take much digging to pull up an image. A crucial weapon in this warfare against the flesh is simply (to put it in computer lingo) "Don't download any unnecessary information to your hard drive!"

Another issue I'd like to address while we're on the subject of "just looking" is that of the "premeditated sin". I like to think that I coined this term, but I'm sure someone else already beat me to it. Not unlike premeditated murder, premeditated sin has a motive, a plan, and a carrying-out of the act itself. When someone commits premeditated murder, there's a continuous thought-out strategy at work. First, there's the motive: "I don't like this guy". Next, there's the plan: "I'll hide behind his car Tuesday night and kill him". Then, there's the act itself: he's dead, he can't be made alive again, this event cannot be undone, the results are final and devastating. Many people are affected in a murder, many people are hurt and, at the very least, the murderer is sought out, captured, sentenced, and punished. "Can't God forgive him?" you may ask. Of course, but that won't prevent or change any of the subsequent consequences of his actions. You see, sin, when thought out and planned, is very much like a pre-planned murder or any pre-planned crime for that matter. "But I never committed or planned out a sin," you might say. Well, let's look at a scenario and see if it rings any bells with you. There's this very attractive young lady working at your local coffee shop on Mondays. She's very friendly and loves to "small talk" whenever you stop in. She's also been known to dress very scantily, especially in the summer. Now you're a married man and don't have the excuse of looking for a wife, but you make sure on Mondays that you look a little neater, a little more hip, and even when your work for that day doesn't put you in that particular area, you still go out of your way to drop in for coffee. Do you talk about salvation? And would you be embarrassed if the person next in line knew you and asked you a spiritual question in front of this young lady? Do you look forward to seeing this person just a little? Do you ever revisit a memory of giving her your coffee order in the past? My friend, if you've ever been involved in anything like this (or anything similar to this) then you've been involved in a premeditated sin. A situation like this one might seem like harmless flirting, but given the proper fuel and spark, it can without warning develop into disaster. Maybe it might take years, but men who find themselves trapped in the middle of a disastrous situation will tell you it all started with a "seemingly" harmless flirtation. It can and does happen every day. Don't be a part of it! Run away from it! Don't initiate it! When you spot a situation that might be (or even has the appearance of) a questionable circumstance for you to be in or around, flee! Resist it and run to the Lord in prayer, *2Ch 7:14 If my people, which are called by my name, shall humble themselves, and pray, and seek my face, and turn from their wicked ways; then will I hear from heaven, and will forgive their sin,* Unfortunately we men have a weakness for flattery and a pretty face. Put the two together and we turn into pathetic fools. Be aware of a woman with a flattering tongue the Bible says, *Pr 7:21 With her much fair speech she caused him to yield, with the flattering of her lips she forced him. Pr 7:22 He goeth after her straightway, as an ox goeth to the slaughter, or as a fool to the correction of the stocks;*

Don't place yourself in compromising situations with no way of escape. Something that might be as innocent as driving home your seventeen-year-old babysitter can develop into disaster when you combine your weakness for the flesh with that of a master deceiver, Satan, who knows how to use that weakness against you and is only too delighted to do so. Remember you are no match for Satan and your old sin nature. Alone, you cannot do anything. But in the Spirit through Christ, you can overcome! You don't see recovered alcoholics hanging out in bars. They know better. They know how easy the fall can be. They've admitted, "I have a problem, I'm an alcoholic!" Can you admit it? Can you admit that you have a problem with the sins of the flesh? Just as the reformed drinker knows that he is just one drink away from falling, you must be ever aware of your weakness and forever be on your guard. Never fall into the devil's trap of fooling yourself into thinking that you're better now and that you can handle the situation that you're contemplating going into. You cant!

CHAPTER 3

Samson, Solomon, and David: men of like passions — ***Romans 3:10***

One of the first feelings I can remember about my realization that I had a problem was "I'm the only one like this; no one can have such thoughts and still be a Christian." You can just imagine how devastated and lost I felt. And it's not like it's one of those things that you bring up in daily conversation. But in actuality, that was my biggest mistake. I was always afraid to say anything because I was convinced that I was the only one having this struggle. Adding to my dilemma was the fact that I held important positions in my local church, and also that I was looked-up-to by younger Christians as a "model Christian". "So how could I possibly slip and let my guard down? How could I risk being found out?" These were some of my distressing thoughts at that time. I thank God for his compassionate Word! Through His Word He lifted me up and out of my mental anguish. The Bible can be such a refuge in times of trouble and doubt! No matter what sin you're in, the Bible has it covered: from lying to the perverseness of "beastiality". It's all covered. You can just imagine my relief when I found out that there were men in the Bible who were just like me: men who were caught up in the very same struggle as I. And these men weren't just any men, they were men who held positions of great prominence and who were very close to God.

Let's start with Samson. Oh, what a man! Although he was a man of God and an appointed Judge of Israel for twenty years, he was also just a natural man to whom I can relate. In case you are not entirely familiar with the story, let me briefly turn back the pages of time, back to the year 1161 BC. Samson, which means like the sun was the son of Manoah from the town of Zorah. Samson was born under the vow of a Nazarene. He was endowed, by God, with supernatural powers in order to deliver God's people from the bondage of the Philistines. Now you would think that a man like this would be a very spiritual and holy person. On the contrary. I found that he was a lot like me. Now I'm not saying that I've been endowed with super-human strength. What I am saying is that Samson, like me, was both a man of God, and at the same time, was a man that still had a stumbling block to overcome. Yes, Samson was, shall I say in today's vernacular, a skirt chaser. He had a weakness for pretty women and it often brought him trouble. The Bible doesn't give us much information about his personal thoughts, but I'm sure he fought a spiritual battle to overcome it. It wasn't like he didn't know that it was wrong. After all, he was a judge appointed by God Himself! Samson knew what was wrong and what was right. He also knew the consequences of his actions, and in the end, he paid the price. He forfeited his strength, his sight, and subsequently, his life. Sad to say, it only took the seduction of one women to bring this mighty man down. After reading the account of his betrayal by Delilah, you might say, Hey! Was this guy stupid or something. Think carefully. I'm certain we can all appreciate the power of a sensual beautiful woman and how all rationale can go right out the window. You know, there's a reason the Lord speaks so often in His Word about the snares of a beautiful woman. Now I know that a lot of people choose to view the Bible as being anti-female, but all that the Lord is saying is that a man can be easily brought down by the sensual words of certain women (not all women, but some). So He says, Watch out! Be aware, guys! Don't put yourselves in such a situation. Samson grew up in a Godly home and in a time when family values were the norm, but he still fell prey to the flesh. So for us who are living in today's world of lack of values, there is little need to explain what we are up against and why it is so very important to listen to God's good advice in the Bible and to heed all of His warning signs.

Another way that the Lord showed me that I was not alone in this was by having me encounter some Christian men who actually had the very same struggle. I remember being surprised to hear even a pastor and then a missionary admit to having the same struggle at some point in his life. So I began to see that other men, both older and younger men alike, had fought with this same sin; and for a while it did give me some peace. But, I "knew" that the Lord still wanted change, and that He was not pleased with my sin. And my attempts at trying to justify my sins were growing thin even to my own mind; so I knew, with a certainty, that I was surely not fooling God in any way, shape, or form with my little justification games. To the natural man in the world, my sins would be viewed as "So what's the big deal?" But you see, being a Christian turns everything around. I'm sure if I were to tell co-workers, or just about any unsaved man, that I'm trying not to look at other women because it's adultery in the eyes of God, they'd probably laugh and think that I was crazy! They'd probably say, "It's OK. You're a guy, and guys like looking when a pretty face strolls by." I can hear them saying, "Lighten up, bud, and just enjoy the view. You Christians are just too darn up-tight." I remember back when Jimmy Carter was President and was handed a loaded question about lusting. When asked if he believed that "just looking" was committing adultery, he responded quickly, "Yes!" Well, you can just imagine the "ribs" and uproar of scoffing that he endured. Yes, the Bible does, indeed, say that. Unfortunately, the country wasn't ready for a Christian President and his downward spiral of unpopularity continued, and he was gone from the scene as quickly as he had appeared. I would not want to be in the shoes of those who persecuted him; God knows all and vengeance is, indeed, His.

All through the Bible we find people just like you and me, all struggling with one sin or another. Remember King Solomon and his great fall into apostasy, when he had fallen to such a gut-wrenching low that he was led by his anguish to pen these words: *Oh, vanity of vanities; all is vanity!* Solomon learned that, apart from total devotion and obedience to God, only lies despair and sorrow. Solomon had it all and was given the wisdom of God to boot. Yet, even in his God-given position and abundance of blessings, he still became, should I say, distracted, lost his focus. And by what force did this come about? Was it sickness or war or famine? No, that would have been all a piece of cake for a man like Solomon. No, it was the simple sin of taking his eyes off the Lord and putting them on something else: in his case, not one, but many, women. You see Solomon's case is a little different, but then again, the same in a way. Solomon had, in today's words, a mid-life crisis. He was not happy. He had attained all that there was to attain. He had already tried all that this world could offer: money, fame, notoriety. So what was left to try, but sexual pleasures. Solomon did not just have one or two, or even three woman, but hundreds! Hey, it just goes to prove that if Solomon, with all these so-called advantages, couldn't find happiness and joy, then no one can. But then true happiness and joy, as Solomon eventually found out, only comes from being in fellowship with God — total devotion and obedience to Him! I recommend reading the Book of Ecclesiastes. Besides its revelations about the emptiness of sexual sin, it also covers all the emptiness of life itself when one attempts to live it apart from total fellowship with God.

Now let's take a look at Solomon's father, King David. He, indeed, knew all about the lust of the flesh — he was even driven so far as to commit murder because of it. And he, indeed, paid the price by losing his son and by suffering the agony, the separation, and the wrenching pain of grieving God. His words ring true even today: *Against Thee, and only Thee, have I sinned.* King David is a classic example of giving in to the lust of the flesh. If ever there was a textbook scenario of chain of events, this is it. David was a man well loved and admired. He had a loving wife, fair to look upon. He had the favor of the Lord Himself and was even called the apple of God's eye. Yet, he fell. Let's walk through this classic case and take a look at the web of entanglements that grew deeper and deeper with every turn.

So David just happens to be glancing off in the distance one night and to his surprise his eyes innocently fall upon a beautiful young lady, lets say, taking a bath, and, of course, naked. Pitfall Number One: (which David failed to avoid) If you think that there may be something out there to look at that you shouldn't, don't! That was David's first mistake. Man always rationalizes and says "It's 'just looking', right? What's the harm?" Well, we all know the answer to that one — Pitfall Number Two: (and it is always the same) the lusting itself, "I want her". And in David's case, since he was King and all, he could have whatever he wanted, and so he did! And that was Pitfall Number Three: the act itself from which there is no point of return.

Just for the record, I'd like to clear up all the fuss about what defines the act. Is it intercourse only? Is it OK as long as you don't touch the genitals or whatever? Let's just ask the Authority! In Matthew 5:27 and 28, God in His Word says *"Ye have heard that it was said by them of old time, Thou shalt not commit adultery: but I say unto you, that whosoever looketh on a woman to lust after her hath committed adultery with her already in his heart."* So, since lusting in your heart is the same as the act itself, then brother, you don't have a leg to stand on. It's all out! Kissing, touching, petting of any kind, even just talking flirtatiously is a no no. Now getting back to David. Was it worth the five, ten, maybe fifteen minutes of pleasure? David knew all too well that it was not, and he paid dearly for giving in to his old sin nature. Did God ever stop loving him? No! Never! But, the Lord is a just judge and at times he will do just that, He will chastise us. He has to, because He is a loving Father! Proverbs 3:11 and 12 instructs us: *"My son, despise not the chastening of the Lord; neither be weary of His correction: for whom the Lord loveth He correcteth; even as a father the son in whom he delighteth."*

We also read in Romans 7:19,24,25 of Paul and his definitive struggle with his old sin nature, *"For the good that I would I do not: but the evil which I would not, that I do. O wretched man that I am! Who shall deliver me from the body of this death? I thank God through Jesus Christ our Lord. So then with the mind I myself serve the law of God; but with the flesh the law of sin."* So for anyone to say that they have never struggled against a particular sin is to deny the very fact of one's fallen state and to declare our Lord's sacrifice on the cross of Golgotha as being all in vain. No, we in today's world, are not so different from the men of Biblical times, and nothing we can do or think today, can ever take the Lord by surprise! God knows exactly how depraved we can be, and more importantly for us, He knows exactly how to aid and abet us when we turn to Him for our help!

Oh, if we would only learn from the mighty men of scriptures and heed their words, we would be spared much anguish and heartache. Oh, to be in the perfect will of God! What great joy close fellowship with our Lord can bring! Nothing else can compare — not any person, place, nor thing on this planet! So let's learn from Samson, Solomon, and David and their fall; for when we do fall, for certainty, it is always away — away from the Lord. For what shall a man profit if he gain the whole world yet lose his own soul? So, fight the fight! Look towards the prize! Always think eternally, never earthly. Proverbs 14:4 says *"Where there is no ox the crib is clean, but much work comes by the strength of an ox".*

Yes, you could sit back and declare it's too hard, the road too steep, the burden too heavy (and you might even get by in this world without too much grief because of the hardness of your heart) but, what will be the price that you will have to pay? Think of the price Samson, Solomon, and David paid for their impulsiveness! And think, who else might suffer and endure hardship because of your selfish existence? The children who never knew their dad and carried with them that emptiness and handed it down unto their children? It may seem to you that your personal acts have no far-reaching impact on anyone. However, in the overall picture your actions have great impact! One scenario might be The son you never nurtured does likewise to his son, and by this fact his son chooses a road that causes hurt and pain to others in his path. Look at David and his son Solomon . My friend, it can go on and on. You are important! In fact, you are crucially important! And you are especially important in the economy of God's purpose! What road will you travel and for whom will you travel it?

CHAPTER 4

Where there's smoke there's fire ,The danger signs

Proverbs 6:27,28,29

One thing I hate is the flu! When winter starts to creep on in, I start to get the pre-flu jitters. I just don't want to get it. I know the symptoms and I'm forever on the look-out for them. Maybe you can say I'm a hypochondriac. Well, so be it. If I start to feel a little achy or a little warm, I start to get nervous. "Oh no, it's coming!" I know the symptoms. I can see it coming.   I also don't like being around people who have it. "Please don't sneeze on me! Please don't get too close to me when we're talking." I even know how to spot a person who already has it. I just want to get away! This might seem mean for a Christian to think this way; but yes, the flesh is weak. I'm a protectionist. I think, in reality, we all are to one point or another. I think paranoia is not given enough credit. I remember reading a comic strip one day. It was about a patient and his psychiatrist. The patient was lying on the couch and the psychiatrist was sitting with his note pad. The caption read, "You're not paranoid Mr. Jones. People really are out to get you." Now I'm not saying that we should walk around totally in a state of fear; but let's face it, as Christians we are (as the Bible points out in Ephesians 6) in a spiritual battle and Satan and his demons are out to trip us up.

> *Finally, my brethren, be strong in the Lord, and in the power of His might. Put on the whole armour of God, that ye may be able to stand against the wiles of the devil. For we wrestle not against flesh and blood, but against principalities against powers, against the rulers of the darkness of this world, against spiritual wickedness in high places. Wherefore take unto you the whole armour of God, that ye may be able to withstand in the evil day.* **Ephesians 6:10-13a**

Like me with my fear of the flu, it's definitely a prudent fear; there's no disputing it. Staying away from what can hurt you is only logical. The trick is knowing your own personal area of weakness. Where can the enemy get a foothold? How much is too much and is there an escape hatch? How do I get myself out of here? Brother, I think the biggest mistake we can make is thinking that we are so spiritually mature that we can handle any situation. I've made that fatal mistake. It's so easy. We have to remember who and what we are up against. I've heard it put this way. Take the person with the highest IQ in the world, just as an example let's say it is 200 while the devils IQ may be 5000. Do you think you're any match? He's 500 times faster than the quickest modem. He has 1200 times more memory than the best "Hard drive". You can't possibly hope to outwit him. Remember, next to the Lord God, he's the most powerful being there is. So what do we do? Well, let's start off with a simple list of danger areas, a simple list of things you might catch yourself doing, "Flu symptoms" if you would. As you read the following list of symptoms reflect back, and if you're like most normal red-blooded men many of these will seem all too familiar to you.

#1. When on the beach do you find it hard to keep your eyes on your wife and kids? Are you easily distracted by the passing of a pretty woman?

#2. When watching TV, do you sometimes find yourself channel surfing and stopping for a quick look at a sexy commercial or program and have a hard time passing them by?

#3. Have you ever watched a scrambled cable channel that was showing an "R" or "X"-rated movie trying to make out the picture through the lines?

#4. When in a waiting room, do you find yourself looking through all the magazines for sexy ads and articles, and trying not to let anyone know what you're looking at?

#5. Do you nonchalantly browse through the Victoria's Secret catalog when it comes in the mail?

#6. Do you ever give an adult book or adult video store a second look and wonder, even for a second, "Gee! I bet I could run in there quick and no one would ever find out?"

#7. Did you ever find yourself in a situation where a pornographic magazine was staring you in the face and you just had to look?

#8. Do you have the Play Boy channel?

#9. Do you pick out movies that are known to have (even brief) nudity?

#10. Are you losing interest in your wife and are you no longer enjoying her physically?

#11. Do you find yourself flirting with a woman at the slightest sign of her showing an interest?

#12. Have you ever wondered or fantasized about other women?

My friend, if you answered "Yes" to even one of these, then you have had a symptom of the sin that the Bible calls "The lust of the flesh"; and yes, the flesh is weak. So what do you do? For starters, don't go where the fish are biting. Don't look for trouble. "Do you mean that I can never go to the beach again?" Yes, that's exactly what I mean; maybe not forever, but at least until you—or more correctly, until you allow God to—break the strong hold. You can't do it by will power, remember. The day you try will be the day Satan has the beach loaded with the best; and just when you think you can handle anything, that's when Satan calls out the skinny dipper.

There are so many pitfalls to watch out for. There is so much wisdom needed. Looking at my own life, I've discovered my many weak areas and God has shown me what situations I should avoid like the plague! I remember teaching some classes one time which included several young and older women. It was quite often that the teaching atmosphere would quickly "go south" with just a single suggestive remark. Before I knew it, I was fanning the flames instead of quenching them. It's not always "looking" that can get you into trouble. Sometimes all it takes is a single word to set your old sin nature into motion. The workplace is probably the most difficult and dangerous area. It doesn't really matter if you're a blue- or a white-collar worker. If there are women around, then trouble can be found. Again, I want to emphasize that the women are not the problem. God gives instruction to men about lust because He knows that woman aren't that effected by it (not as much, I should say, though even that is starting to change; but that's another story). We've all heard it before and it is so true: "Women use sex to get love, and men use love to get sex", sad but true.

Getting back to the work place. My friend, stay away from the water cooler "chit chat"! Stay away from sexual innuendoes! Stay away from any compromising situations! And definitely don't fall for the friendly counselor, "just trying to help her while she's down" trap. Her marriage or her boyfriend problems are none of your business, and distancing yourself is your best defense. If you do have to work closely with a female co-worker always make it a point to let it be known, right from the start, that you are happily married. *Never*, and I mean *NEVER!* go to a female co-worker with your marital problems. And for that matter, you should be only seeking advise from a Christian anyway. And I've also found that just by making it "known" that you are a Christian usually keeps most problems of this type from ever arising. But while we are mentioning Christians, I must give a caution to be on your guard and aware that more and more Christians, unfortunately, are falling into "Christian-Christian" adulterous situations. Know and remember this, "There are NO safe waters!" Even being in church will not make you exempt from having lustful thoughts. When the Bible says that women should dress in a certain manner it was for purpose!

> *In like manner also, that women adorn themselves in modest apparel, with shamefacedness, and sobriety; not with braided hair, or gold, or pearls, or costly array; but (which becometh women professing godliness) with good works. (I Timothy 2:9-10)*

I've heard of many a Youth Leader falling prey to a young teenage girl in his group. That's an especially dangerous mine field. For instance, take a young male Youth Leader away on a camping trip, add a few young impressionable teenage girls with a crush, and you have the potential for major damage—not only to the two people involved, but also to the church, to the families, and to the testimony to the community. This extremely unwise situation has the potential for setting into motion a horrible domino effect destroying everything in its path. My recommendation to anybody is: If you have a weakness in that area, then *Don't! do not! get involved in that ministry!* There are many ways the Lord can use you. There are many avenues of service for the King. Please be honest enough with yourself to know when to say "No". You should be consulting God in prayer, anyway, <u>before</u> you enter into a ministry to see if that is where <u>He</u> wants to use you.

The title of this chapter is "Where there's smoke, there's fire". We have to become expert smoke readers. Just as ignorance of the law is no excuse in the world, ignorance of not seeing smoke is not excusable either. If you possess this stumbling block, this struggle against the lust of the flesh, then you know very well what the smoke looks like.

> *Can a man take fire in his bosom, and his clothes not be burned? Can one go upon hot coals, and his feet not be burned? So he that goeth in to his neighbor's wife; whosoever toucheth her shall not be innocent. (Proverbs 6:27-29)*

And let's not forget, that besides our own sin nature, we still have Satan roaming around "seeking whom he may devour". When you see smoke, don't be a hero! Pull the fire alarm and run! Run as fast as you can, in the opposite direction! Be man enough to admit defeat! Another thing I cannot stress enough is: Be prepared for the battles that may lie ahead. Be prepared for even Christian misconceptions. In fact, I remember one situation in my own life where the "laws of ignition" proved to be Oh so true. I was picking up supplies for work one day and during the drive there I was remembering a fair maiden who was sometimes behind the counter. (Problem one was I did not quench this thought, I just lit the match.) The next thing I knew, I spotted her there and the battle had begun,("don't look, don't look"), I looked, and she sure looked pretty today! (The fuel is being poured out all over the floor.) I could have stopped it even there, but I took that vision with me, lust has taken place, the lit match was tossed, and the flames consumed, how? Well by, one, breaking my fellowship with the Lord and, two, by stifling any spiritual work the Lord might have had in store for me that day. I saw the smoke, I smelled the fumes, I knew the reaction, yet I threw the match.   *O wretched man that I am! who shall deliver me from the body of this death?*   **Romans 7:24**

In your attempt to avoid the temptations of the world, you sometimes might appear to some people as a self-righteous hypocrite. I remember some looks (even sad to say from brothers and sisters in Christ) when I would refuse to rent an "*R*"-rated movie. And I remember the looks that I got from the cable guy when I requested that, in addition to having the Playboy Channel scrambled, that he also would install filters to block out the, Oh so explicit, audio portion of it. I'm in no way a super saint. I'm just trying to put out the fire even before I can smell the smoke. Taking such measures can be humbling I know; but we know what the Lord says about being humble.

> *Submit yourselves therefore to God. Resist the devil, and he will flee from you. Draw nigh to God, and He will draw nigh to you. Cleanse your hands, ye sinners; and purify your hearts, ye double-minded. (James 4:7-8)*

It also helps to have an understanding Christian wife to help you in your struggle. Let me give you a personal example of how an innocent situation can become a seed-bed of sin. Back when I was in the depths of my bondage I became involved in a "virtual" fling with someone without them even knowing it. Many things can be blamed for the events that followed: an old sin nature, discontentment, an overactive imagination, and even Satan himself; all played a part. But above all, the lust of the flesh was the driving sin. I'd also like to make a point at this time: Whenever you're involved in any sin, you'll find that other sins will not be far behind. For instance, if you're under the bondage of stealing, will not lying be close behind? Will not covetousness have a hand in it also? It's kind of like the domino effect. One sin always leads to more. Lying follows just about all of them. In all these areas there's one thing you can count on and that's that Satan is watching wide-eyed and calculating. I know the world has mocked this notion, and the phrase "the Devil made me do it" is all but reserved for kooks and cultists or jokes. But let me tell you this, Satan might not always cause the sin, but he's sure there to urge you on at the slightest inkling of a weak area in your character. That's what happened to me. Many years ago before we were married, my wife became friendly with a woman that she'd met at work. In time they became better and better friends. At that same time I was fighting the spiritual warfare of the flesh. Our relationship was a little bit shaky due to a stressful time we had just gone through and our future was looking dim. This friend of my wife-to-be wasn't anything out of the ordinary. She was of average looks and build and had a pleasant persona. What the "fiery dart" was, was her innocent friendliness to me. I don't even know how it all began, but I found myself believing that she had "a thing" for me, which to this day I'm sure was all in my head. Never-the-less, my sin nature would feed on it, and in turn, would create many a fantasy scenario. She would often compliment me on my looks and always welcomed me with a hearty hug and a kiss which would always last just a millisecond longer than I thought appropriate. Little things like leaning against me by accident, and stuffing money in my back pocket that she had borrowed didn't help either. Now don't think Satan didn't know what was in the wind. I'm sure he had his hand in fanning the flames of desire. As time went by I knew I had a serious problem and that if it went too far it would destroy all of our plans. I also had warring within me the conviction of the Holy Spirit on one side battling my old sin nature on the other. There were times when I would stay in check, but then there were other times when my imagination would run wild. These were the times (I can see His Hand in it clearly now) that God would intercede and pull me out right before I went too far. You see, I actually started to set up situations to place myself around her. I would be Oh, so helpful and friendly under the guise of being a great humanitarian Christian. Did I ever think about her soul and leading her to the Lord? No. Brother, this is exactly where Satan loves to have a believer, totally under his finger and feeling like you have no control over him or yourself. He especially loves it when you start thinking things like: "What kind of Christian am I? How can the Lord ever use me now? I'm such a failure and an evil person." Well, it is true about evil; *"For out of the heart proceed evil thoughts, murders, adulteries, fornications, thefts, false witness, blasphemies" (Matthew 15:19).* But did not Christ die for those very sins? Yes! (And I'll get into that very important fact at greater length later in this book.) Once Satan has you in this defeatist state, it won't be long before you're thinking about running away and giving up on Christianity. Before you know it, Satan will have you thinking things like you have lost your salvation, which God clearly tells us in His Word we cannot possible do. *"My Father, which gave them Me, is greater than all; and no man is able to pluck them out of My Father's hand" (John 10:29).* And pretty soon Satan will have you thinking that suicide is the only way out. The best way out of these foolish fetishes is to think of them as just that. Sit down and ask the Lord to give you a clear head; and then logically envision the unimaginable travesty that would most certainly follow such a foolish endeavor. Think about how it would affect your children, your wife, your testimony, your church, your neighbors, and most importantly, your walk with the Lord. Is it really worth it? You know it's only lust even though Satan tries to convince you it's love. I know you're probably thinking, "I know this is all true, but that still doesn't change the fact of these feelings that I'm having and how to control them." You're absolutely right; and rational thinking has nothing in common with the bondage of sin. Read on.

CHAPTER 5

What's the worst that could happen?

Proverbs 6:26-29

The two dumbest things I ever said, much to my chagrin, pop back into my mind every now and then. Number one, "I'll never be one of those 'Born again Christians' and the second, "What's the worst that could happen?" Out of all the techniques and formulas I give in this book, the one that's so basic and simple and so easily by-passed is this one: Think about your future! For those of you who are familiar with the new Batman movies, remember the first one with Michael Keaton when the detective is talking to Jack Nicholson and says to him, "Think about your future". For some reason that always sticks in my mind. It's so true! We so easily get caught up in the day to day issues of our lives that we just start to lose touch with reality. I know with me, it seems like just yesterday that I was just hanging out with the guys. I was 17 or 18 forever, it seemed. Life was so simple and selfish. Have fun, buy things for yourself, and look at girls. Wow, what happened? Now I'm thirty-five. I'm married with two kids, a home, a demanding job, and, to top it all, I've given my life to the Lord. Talk about radical change! Even though I realize it was a gradual transition, it seems like it happened overnight: the responsibility, and the bills, and the stress, trying to be a good Christian, and still remaining sane. It's scary because I still feel like I'm seventeen some times. I want to call my buddies and go out to play. When you start feeling like this, it's a bad sign, I'm sorry to say. Something's just not right! That's not how the Lord wants you to be thinking. Remember Lot's wife? Looking back means that you're not happy with the future. And if you're not happy with the future, then you're not happy with what the Lord has given you , *I Timothy 6:6 But godliness with contentment is great gain.* You start thinking things like, "What's the worst that could happen? I could have an affair, maybe a quickie. I can't handle the stress and this girl I met really understands me. She makes me feel the way I did back then. I'm really not happy with life. I need a change. Every body's doing it nowadays." Sounds so easy; but let's take a more serious look at the situation. Number one and foremost is you'll be sinning against God! Number two, what about your kids? How will they get along without Dad? And forget about spending quality time with them! Your children will bear the effects of this for the rest of their lives. And how about your wife? She'll have to get full-time work, put the kids in day care and do it all: both mom and dad, homemaker, provider, and spiritual leader. Your children will think it's their fault and blame either themselves or their mother. Forget about your testimony to your neighbors and co-workers and friends! If there was someone who was considering the Lord because of you, you can forget about that now. Forget about your walk with the Lord! Maybe you think if you marry a Christian woman it's OK. Not! Or maybe you think, "Maybe I'll meet a girl who's not saved and I can lead her to the Lord". You know it'll never happen, and even if it did, you're act of leaving your wife was never God's perfect will. Or you might think "Maybe I can stay married, have a girl on the side just for sex, and not hurt anyone". My friend, I can guarantee you one thing: If you think you'll find peace and happiness going this route, you're wrong! What you will find will be: Guilt, bitterness, unhappiness, sorrow, and regret. You will Never be happy! Remember, once it's done, it's done! Things will never be the same again. Yes, God will forgive you if you repent. But don't think He's not going to have to reprimand you. There will be chastisement! To what degree? Only God knows. I know what you're thinking. "How about me? How about my wants and desires? Doesn't God want me happy?" The answer is "Yes" He wants you happy; but, Brother, you and I and the rest of this sin-sick world have to sit back and realize, you are last, God is first, then your wife, then your children. Your responsibility and desire is to please them, and them alone. You are their spiritual leader, provider, and protector. Everything else is secondary at best. Only when these principles are followed will you ever find peace and happiness and contentment. "I've been doing all these things", you say. Have you really? All of them? If you neglect one, then you're guilty of them all , *Job 17:9 The righteous also shall hold on his way, and he that hath clean hands shall be stronger and stronger.* How long have you been doing them? Five years, ten years, fifteen years? It's not long enough. Are you doing them in the Spirit? Are you asking the Lord to help you and empower you? I know all the outs and complaints—believe me, I've had all the same thoughts and feelings. But running away is not the answer.

What does all this have to do with "Girl Watching" and the lust of the flesh? It's all relative. All these things start with looking elsewhere. Maybe you no longer desire your wife. Maybe she's gained a couple of pounds and doesn't look like a girl in a sports car ad. Maybe all you do is fight and argue and you feel you just aren't compatible anymore. Maybe she's too spiritual or not spiritual enough. Maybe it's all your fault, maybe not, but it's a good place to start. *Philippians 1:9 And this I pray, that your love may abound yet more and more in knowledge and in all judgment.* The Bible says that judgment begins in the house of God. Why not begin with yourself.

You know, one of the hardest things to do is to look inward, to tear open your soul and lay it upon the altar. We hear the world always proclaiming how they are "finding themselves" and looking deep inside to "find their soul". That's not what you need. As a Christian, it's completely different, for we start with the heart; and we know from the Bible that the heart of man is desperately wicked. (Ooh that hurts!) Yes, to admit one's ills and deficiencies is not a desirable venture. To dig down into one's secret, private world is a task that takes grander virtue by far. What are our motivations? What makes us do the things we do? Do I really care about this one or that one's well being; or more to the point, do I really care about their salvation? These are cutting introspections I'm sure. But never-the-less, they must be reckoned with. Judgement begins, yes, at the House of God — from within. This means that God wants us to first — before we judge or try to help anyone else — look inside ourselves and judge ourselves. We must determine and admit to ourselves what our sins are; and then immediately confess them to God, bring them to the Throne Room of Grace. "Dear Father, I have sinned, forgive me". You see, until we judge ourselves and stop kidding ourselves, stop telling ourselves that we are fine that it is really the world that is at fault and is causing all of our sins and shortcomings, then we can never be in fellowship with God, which becomes separation from God, which becomes no communication with God, ie: unanswered prayer. At this point we start blaming God for His silence. We proclaim "The Lord has left me, so I will now leave Him. He's not delivering 'nirvana' so I will find my own". Oh how we are so quick to lash out at the Lord, when in reality, we are the one's who left Him, not the other way around. We left when we sinned and refused to confess it, leaving Him no choice but to remain silent to our cries. *"But if we confess our sins, He is faithful and just to forgive us our sins and to cleanse us from all unrighteousness" (I John 1:9).* If we hold iniquity in our hearts, He cannot hear us; not that He "can't", but through "our" actions (sin), He's bound by His own law to not respond. Just ask King David when he cried out "restore the joy of my salvation" King David experienced, in full, what the desolation of broken fellowship with God was like. There is no lonelier place to be, than where God is "not"!

So what can we do? We must get back into fellowship through genuine repentance to our Lord. Ask Him to aid you in revealing your inner faults (sins) and turning from them, in, through, and by faith. "Lord, I'm selfish. Lord, I'm vain. Lord, I hate. Lord, I'm afraid. Lord, I lust. Lord, I need you, for I can't make this life without you!" Forget "macho" and think "humble". *Job 22:29 When men are cast down, then thou shalt say, There is lifting up; and he shall save the humble person.* Exalt the humble, and humble the exalted, (Matthew 23:12). Until you are man enough to humble yourself before God, forget about peace, forget about joy, forget about even one prayer being answered.

The question is not, "What's the worst that could happen?" The question is "What's the worst that won't happen?" You want to play? Then you must play by God's rules. You want to have joy? Then you must attain it God's way. You want to love and desire your wife again? Then just ask Him. With forgiveness on your side, His answer will be "Yes, my child, you can be whole again!" The "worst" that could happen is not what you need. The "best" that God has is what you should desire for yourself. The "best" that He has is what God desires for you!

CHAPTER 6

Be a Wife Watcher

Proverbs 5:18,19

As I mentioned earlier in the "Danger Signs," one danger sign is "a loss of interest or desire for your wife." There are many ways that this can manifest itself, and a lot of times it will go unnoticed under the guise of "men just wanting to get away from the 'old lady'". In my years of working in the world, I've seen it in so many ways, especially for those men in the "blue collar" trades. If you've ever hung around with the guys, be it during lunchtime or around the water cooler to "shoot the breeze," there are probably only limited things you've talked about. You've talked about things like sports, the boss, the latest dirty joke, or your wives. Now as a Christian, none of these things should be part of our water-cooler dialogue, which doesn't really leave too much else to converse about. That's also why, if you are living for the Lord at work, you probably won't be all that liked. So be it. If you're not good at witnessing, like myself, this is one way of "letting your light so shine." Getting back to the "old lady" jokes, it's just not right! It's unspiritual and a sign that something isn't copacetic at home. Men, if we don't like our wives it won't be long before they no longer seem attractive to us.It won't be long before we stop kissing, then touching, and then a complete loss of desire for them in any way.. If all this continues unchecked for too long, it won't be long before the "old lady" becomes just that. If you don't or won't like her, you will, in short, no longer love her. And my friend, that is a sin! I know, I've heard them all before; I've said them all before: "She's such a nag. She's just not the woman I married. She gained too much weight. I'm just not attracted any more. She won't do what I want. She doesn't satisfy me. I need a change, someone who cares about me, someone who makes me feel young again." My friend, in case you haven't realized it, there's a pattern here. "I," "I," seems to appear quite often and the "I's" have it. I know what you're thinking: "You 'know' it's true and that it's wrong, but it still doesn't change the fact that you want to be happy wether it's a sin or not." You know what? God wants you happy too. Yes, it's true. He doesn't want you living a life of depression and discontentment. The problem is that you think you need one thing to make you happy and God " knows" you need something else. Who are you going to believe? You may not believe it, but you can love your wife and you can be happy, and yes, she can become desirable to you once again. Remember, you once loved her and enjoyed her, and even if you never did, you can. Not on your own and not your way, but God's way. And don't tell me you already tried, you never really did. The fact that you're reading this book tells me that you haven't.

She "can" understand you . She "can" please you like you've never thought. You "can" be happy, and yes, it's OK to passionately "crave" your wife, and you should. I don't care what your wife looks like, wether she is fat or skinny or even if she hates sex itself, this can all change. The amazing thing is that you can't change her or make her what you want, just as she can't change you or make you into what she wants. Only God can. My friend, there is no "catch" or "magic formula." There's only the Bible. There's only God's way, and it all begins with you "wanting it." You see, God won't force us into anything. We are not puppets, or else we would all have perfect lives and perfect marriages and be living a sinless life. We have free will. We can choose to ask God to change us or we can choose to live in our sinful carnal life apart from God's perfect will and His abundant blessings. Throughout this book, one constant remains true: If you don't want to change, if you don't want to give your life over to the Lord, it will never ever happen. Just because you enjoy "Girl Watching" doesn't mean you don't want to stop. Just like my smoking problem I had; I really enjoyed it, and still sometimes desire it . The difference was that I "knew" that it was killing me. I "knew" God wasn't pleased. And I "knew" I had to stop. I couldn't, but God could. He just needs the "OK" from us and the desire to stop. Also, remember that a strong willpower has nothing to do with it. Willpower never overcame any sin. Only a repentant heart and the working of the Holy Spirit will suffice. Willpower says "I can do it," and "I"can do, says "God can't", and that has "pride" written all over it and we all know how God feels about pride. Brother, remember this, "When God looks at you and your wife, He sees a beautiful couple "made in the image of God." He sees His perfect will being fulfilled. And even when you're together in the physical way, God sees a wonderful joining of His creation with no "sin." I know, we all have a hard time thinking of the Lord and being intimate with our wives, but that's just plain wrong and is a tool of Satan. Did you know that the Lord puts His complete blessing and full approval on your lovemaking. There's nothing wrong or dirty, and there's nothing to hide. He created sex and designed both the male and female body to feel and emote with unrestrained ecstasy. Only Satan and the fallen world have corrupted it into something dirty and perverted. Physical beauty was never a prerequisite for a fulfilling sexual experience. The only requirement was that it be within the bonds of matrimony, between a man and a women in love. Satan has corrupted this by placing lies of sexual fulfillment only through perfect sexy "super models" and only out of the bonds and blessing of Holy Matrimony. He's made us believe that our wives can never fulfill us, that we need a super vixen from a porno ad to really complete our desires. He's made us believe that marriage ruins the excitement and takes away from the relationship. He's lied and told us that, "If there is a God His only desire is to take away your fun and make your life miserable." From TV, to motion pictures, to advertising, to music, it's all a constant daily bombardment of sex and perversion and "self-only" gratification with no room for God or selflessness. Marriage is made to seem like the major problem, and good sex the only reason for living. It doesn't take long before even the strongest Christian will fold and start to compromise and then eventually believe the lies of Satan. Ill tell you Brother, there's never been an age with so much temptation and acceptance of evil, and it is difficult for a young man today, especially young teenagers, but it is "Not" impossible. You have to want to please the Lord and not count the cost. This world will call you a fool for sure, but the rewards, whether on earth or in Heaven will out weigh any persecution in this immoral and Satan-led world. What will it be? Who will you follow? Is it all worth the minutes of godless lust and certain un-fulfillment, the broken testimony, the destruction of your family and the almost certainty that your children will carry on your lifestyle and in turn fall away from Jesus and His Word.

So how do we start? What's the first move? It's simple, yet hard. The simple part is first, making a total "commitment" to Christ — Believing in and accepting Jesus as your personal Lord and Savior. Repenting of all your sins and becoming Born Again. Asking for His help and admitting you're a sinner who can't save or help himself. And then asking God daily, in prayer, to give you the strength and wisdom and direction to live a life that is pleasing unto him. Make your request unto Him in true faith. Ask Him to give you victory. Don't ask Him to make your wife sexier, ask Him that you would find her desirable, as she is. Don't ask Him to change her attitude towards sex, ask Him that He would change yours. Don't ask for good "sex," ask how to "give" good "love". Love your wife like the Bible says, and you will see a new woman being created before your very eyes. Fantasize only of her, and your desires will be fulfilled. Treat her like you did when she was the young girl you fell in love with and she will become that young girl again. Love her, Love her, Love her! And if you can't, ask God to help you. I had a particularly hard time with this myself. First I didn't like her, then I started to not love her. It was hard because I really didn't even "want" to love her and had to start way back and ask God to "Help" me "want" to want to love her. I know it sounds childish but it was a fact that I had to deal with before any progress could be made. All of these areas are "counter- canceling," meaning that, when one aspect starts to come under control, other areas that were problems will correct themselves. Example: When you start to desire your wife physically and emotionally you will start to not desire other women and long for the time to pass when you can make love to her again. You know, I don't even like that term: "Make Love", even though I use it myself. The only one who can "make" love (create it) is the Lord. We, as His children, can only enjoy love — the love and physical satisfaction that He made possible between a husband and wife.

These are all the easy things. The hard part is yours, and that is to "sincerely desire" the change. To not grow impatient and give up. That's the hard part, but

God will even help you with that. Do you really want Godly contentment and joy or the weakness of sin for a season? Love your wife, really love her, even when nothing's happening. Even if it seems to be getting worse. Remember, the devil doesn't want your marriage and testimony to grow. He'll be there. You can count on it. But so will the Lord! Fight the good fight and the spoils of the battle will be yours! ***Proverbs 5:18,19*** *Let thy fountain be blessed: and rejoice with the wife of thy youth. Let her be as the loving hind and pleasant roe; let her breasts satisfy thee at all times; and be thou ravished always with her love.*

CHAPTER 7

Wives, SOS **Ephesians 5:22 and Proverbs 31:25**

This is probably one of the hardest chapters to write. Unfortunately, it's only difficult because of what society has become. How can I speak to wives Biblically without offending someone in this age where people are quick to censor you for not being, of all things, "politically correct". It's so frustrating! Oh how it churns me up when I see the mass confusion that Satan has so deviously and cunningly created: black is white, white is black; right appears to be wrong, and wrong appears to be right; and God help you if you dare to cut against the grain! The women's movement which started out for the good has done more harm then ever dreamed. The mere fact that I have to go through all these apologetics to address a particular issue proves it. It's very simple. The wife of the Bible is an alien creature to this lost and dying world. Her magnificent role in the economy of God has been ostracized as archaic and totally out of touch and dated. But the fact is, this world is dying a quick death. The harder we try to show our wisdom and intellect the more we fall. The wedding ceremony today is a complete farce. It has become no more than a means to have an expensive party showing how much of a spectacle you can create for your friends. It has no spiritual significance, no honor nor commitment, no sacrifice or allowances for the good of the other partner. Prenuptial agreements have become the norm . Staying together is no longer expected. If you make it to five years the world says you are to consider yourself a champion of compromise. One, two, three, or even four divorces are not uncommon and are often boasted about like a prized trophy. The wedding vows have been tailored to fit today's political atmosphere with God being given only a symbolic, if any, significance at all. Our children are being raised by everyone except the parents; and if there is one of the parents, you can bet it's not Dad . And even when there is a father figure around, he's more of a fixture than a relevant part of the unit. Just watch any TV sitcom with a Dad-person and it's easy to see why Dad has become the buffoon of the nineties. He never has a brain and most assuredly is never in control of more than a TV channel-changing device. We've become a society where every role is completely opposite to its created design and purpose. If our new-found so-called personal freedoms and intelligence are so superior to God's, then why is there such a mess out there?

My friend, there is a plan, there is a system that works. Life is not just having a good time and taking care of my needs. It never was and can never be. So what are our roles? Where's the solution to it all? Well, if you're a blood-bought child of the living God you have one foot in the right direction and that direction is The Way, the only Way: Jesus, Jesus, and Jesus! And He is The Living Word—the

Bible. It's our textbook for existence on this planet. There is no other way! Many other paths may spark one's interest, but none but Jesus can ever satisfy our every need and save our soul!

Wives, if you love your husband, if you desire peace and success for your family, if doing what God wants is more important than anything, then please come quickly to the call of this *SOS* signal. Before we get into how you can help your husband, and in turn your family, I'd like to lay some important groundwork and make sure that you know that you as the wife are not a slave to your husband, you are not less than him nor of less importance! If you're a believer, then you're a child of God. You are a special and integral part of God's plan for your marriage!

> *Who can find a virtuous woman? For her price is far above rubies. Strength and honor are her clothing; and she shall rejoice in time to come.* **(Proverbs 31:10,25)**

> *For this cause shall a man leave his father and mother, and shall be joined unto his wife, and they two shall be one flesh.* **(Ephesians 5:31)**

I find that if we look at the Trinity we find a good example of the man-woman relationship to each other and to the Lord. For starters, let's ask this question: Who is more important? The Father, the Son, or the Holy Spirit? The answer: They are all One, yet serve in different capacities. One doesn't operate without the Other. Yet there has to be a Head. One teaches, One intercedes, One has authority yet all are equal many functions with one purpose. The Bible gives us the example of the body of Christ . *"For as we have many members in one body, and all members have not the same office"* **(Romans 12:4)**. Can the hand do as good of a job of walking as the foot can? Can the nose see? Can the eyes hear? Are they all equal in importance? Of course. When they work together, the job gets done magnificently. If one was to attempt to do the other's job, what would you have? Chaos! Why is it then so hard to apply this principle to a marriage. Well for one, and probably the most prevalent, is "Pride". What does the Bible say about it? *"Pride goeth before destruction, and a haughty spirit before a fall"* **(Proverbs 16:18)**. When pride is in action, all is lost. The will of God cannot operate when pride is afoot. *"Husbands, love your wives." "Wives, submit yourselves unto your own husbands"* **(Colossians 3:19a,18a)**. Oh how beautiful and loving a marriage is when these two principles are followed. When these simple principles are applied, things start to happen. When we become self-centered and think only of ourselves, our focus is off of Jesus. Think of your marriage as the proverbial pyramid with Christ being the Head and you and your husband being the two lower corners. The closer we get to Jesus, the closer we get to each other. Keep your eyes on Christ and on the other partner's needs and your needs will be met through the inner peace that only Christ can bring. Wives, you and your husbands are completely different creatures; if it were not so, God would have not needed to create the two. As your husband can't figure you out, neither can you him. But we can try. A man is a sexually-driven machine. As much as you would like to think that he only has eyes for you, it just isn't true. Now I'm not saying that he doesn't love you and you alone; what I am saying is that he can easily be attracted to a passing woman. His sex drive is driven by sight and not emotion. You can talk to him about how much you love him till you're blue in the face, but it's only when he physically sees you or touches your body that he experiences arousal. This need unfortunately does not just come once in a while but is with him every minute of every hour from puberty till death. I'm not saying all men are to this degree, but if you're reading this book then you probably have a husband that fits into this category. If he's having a struggle in this area, then it's important that you understand these emotions. Did you ever feel a sneeze coming on and no matter what you did it could not be stifled until the actual sneeze itself? Well, in a lot of ways your husband's sexual activity works in this manner. The more aroused he gets, whether by you or someone else, the greater the need to deflate it will become. In some cases the desires can become so strong that rational thinking becomes scarce. It doesn't mean your husband is having an affair. All it takes is a seductive TV commercial or a passing girl in a short dress. Now let it be known that I'm not saying these things are acceptable. Each time he gives in to these thoughts, it's sin. It's completely inexcusable to God and is the equivalent to committing adultery.

Ye have heard that it was said by them of old time, Thou shalt not commit adultery: but I say unto you, that whosoever looketh on a woman to lust after he hath committed adultery with her already in his heart. (Matthew 5:27-28)

But the fact is, these things do occur every day, and I challenge any man who denies it. Simply, if your husband has a problem in this area, he probably was exposed to a lot of pornography as a child and has acquired a thought pattern that is difficult to break. To him a women was always portrayed as this sexual nymphomaniac, spandex-clad diva whose only desire in life is giving sexual favors to every man she sees. Abhorrent as it may seem, it's a truth worth considering. He needs help, maybe even professional but that professional must be a Christian Believer. But before you sign him up, lets not forget the Wonderful Counselor, the Lord Jesus!

For unto us a child is born, unto us a Son is given: and the government shall be upon His shoulder: and His Name shall be called

Wonderful, Counselor, The Mighty God, The Everlasting Father, The Prince of Peace. (Isaiah 9:6)

Please, if you do anything for your husband, begin with heartfelt prayer. Of all the advice I can give you, this, I know, can move a mountain! Consult the Wonderful Counselor. Ask for His guidance, strength, and help! Pray "together" with your husband. Together — you and your husband — get down on your knees, ask God to give your husband the victory over this sin. *"Again I say unto you, That if two of you shall agree on earth as touching any thing that they shall ask, it shall be done for them of my Father which is in heaven" (Matthew 18:19).*

So in what other ways, as the Christian wife, can you help? For starters, you can give yourself more credit than you probably are. How do you feel about yourself? Do you think you're pretty? Do you think you are desirable to your husband; or are you ashamed of what God has created? It's just amazing to me what women think they need to attract their man. A perfect figure with flowing blond hair, skin without a blemish or wrinkle is not what's missing. Listen, a man with a weakness for the flesh is easily aroused. You'd be surprised at what little it takes to spark your husband's interest. A sexy voice of provocative or suggestive dialogue can be all that's required from you to get your husband's attention on you (as opposed to where it should not be) and thus keep your husband in fellowship with God as opposed to out of fellowship. The one thing I find that hinders a lot of Christian women is that, being a Christian woman, you feel uncomfortable speaking, thinking, and doing things of the sexual nature. Please remember this important fact: you are married, this is your husband, and the sexual union was created, designed and ordained of God: *Let her be as the loving hind and pleasant roe; let her breasts satisfy thee at all times; and be thou ravished always with her love" (Proverbs 5:18-19). "Marriage is honorable in all, and the bed undefiled" (Hebrews 13:4a).* So you see, it's OK! Your body is his, for his pleasure; and his body is yours, for you. Did you ever pray to become a good lover? Did you ever ask the Lord to help you please your husband? Before you make love, pray! Ask God to bless this holy union tonight. You can't imagine what delights are in store for you when you are praying to please your husband and he is praying to please you. If you think it's improper to speak to God this way, then you don't have the relationship with Him that you should. Hey, if you can tell your best girl friend about your sexual relations, you should be able to tell the Lord. It's not like He doesn't know what's going on. He sees you all the time, and from the inside out, from upside down. Once you've overcome these barriers, you will find it more and more comfortable to deal with these matters. Start by asking your husband what his fantasies are? What does he like? What does he dislike? What turns him off? Surprise him one day by planning a sexual encounter. A unexpected grab on the way out the door for work will keep him going all day. Best of all is that he'll be fantasizing about you! Try greeting him at the door one day with only a T-shirt. No matter what your body's shape, he'll find it attractive. Starting him on the road to(**"*lusting*" see note 1**) after you is the first step to the healing of your marriage.

Another question often asked is, "Do I just fake it? Do I just say 'yes' every time he's a little frisky? And how about me? Am I just a sex slave, a prostitute? When do my needs get met?" These are all good questions and the answers are very simple. Did Jesus say to the Father "What's in this for Me? I'll die for them when they die for Me. I'm doing all the giving and it doesn't appear that I'm going to receive anything for my efforts. Why bother? Of course He didn't. You could say Well, I'm not Jesus. That's true. But you are married and you made a promise to God the day you were married. Do you believe what the Bible says about the husband-wife relationship? Lets look at it another way. Do you love your husband? Do you love the Lord? The choice is simple: either your husband can lust after you or lust after someone else. He can either look forward to coming home or look forward to leaving. If you wait till he starts loving you and doing his part you might be waiting a long tribulatory time. All these things don't make you all to blame and your husband a saint. If he's having this problem, he's in big time sin. You can help or you can watch him fall. When we follow the Lord's way with a pure heart, God will reward us. You'll be surprised in the changes you'll see in your man. He'll start loving you more and, yes, even start to try to fulfill your sexual and emotional needs. Men need respect, women need love. One won't come without the other. Someone's got to give.

Here's a couple more tips. A woman can probably go weeks, if not months, without sexual relief. A man, on the other hand, could probable have sex two times a day, easy! Do you see a problem? I know it's tough in today's crazy fast-paced world, but try. Try twice a week, and don't expect an elaborate love scene. As selfish as it might seem, a man needs to relieve himself. It's a physical thing, not emotional. Just let him know that you'd like to be taken care of once in a while also the way you want it soft music and romance or what ever you like. Pray for him and for yourself. I can't stress this enough! You can't do this of yourself, you need God!

I also have a list of don'ts. Number one being, don't rent movies for the weekend that have any sexual content. The Bible calls this a stumbling block. I find myself safest watching "G"-rated movies. If going to the local beach with scantily clad women is turning his head, just don't go. There is life after "Bay Watch". You don't have to verbally correct him, simply slowly change your recreational habits. Please, spend time with other believers. Fellowship is the key! The less time spent associating with things of this sin-sick world, the better off both of you will be. Encourage him to get involved in a hobby of some sort (not girl watching). Encourage him to spend more time with the family than with the "unsaved guys". Do all these things with a loving heart, never with judgment or condemnation. If it's not working, then pray that God would change these habits. Another bad "no no" is promising him sex and then changing your mind later in the day or week. We men are like children in a lot of ways. That thought of a future encounter with our wives can get us through a whole week. Please, most of all, don't talk about the day's problems and the leaky sink when love making is in progress. The bedroom, or whatever room for that matter, should become a sanctuary for that one purpose of pleasing each other, not talking shop. Admire his body and tell him what turns you on about him. Again, a simple word placed at the proper time can work wonders. Another don't is don't joke around in front of other people about his problem. One word here can destroy months of good progress. Also, love your own body, take care of it. If you love it, then he will to. Don't expect results in one night, and don't go too far too soon. Take it slow and expect nothing in return except to know and be reassured that, as far as " you" yourself and your "own" personal relationship with God is concerned, " you" are doing God's will.

> *Trust in the Lord, and do good; so shalt thou dwell in the land, and verily thou shalt be fed. Delight thyself also in the Lord; and He shall give thee the desires of thine heart. Commit thy way unto the Lord; trust also in Him; and He shall bring it to pass.* **(Proverbs 37:3-5)**

> *Now our Lord Jesus Christ Himself, and God, even our Father, which hath loved us, and hath given us everlasting consolation, and good hope through grace. Comfort your hearts, and stablish you in every good word and work.* **(II Thessalonians 2:16-17)**

What can I say ladies, I know it's a lot of give, give, give. My sister in Christ, it might be a hard road or it might turn around in a week. Remember this, lust of the flesh is a powerful addiction that was many years in the making before you ever came along. It's going to take a lot to break it. Whether the problem is gambling, lying, covetousness, or girl watching, they are all strong holds. If left unchecked, it won't be long until they are footholds. After that they soon become fortresses, which we all know are walls of solid rock.

> ***note (1)*** *Lust is a sin no matter how you look at it. But since the word "lust" is a word that holds such an "intensity of feelings", a word that we men understand as "super super passionately desiring" when it comes to a woman, I am going to use "poetic license", to get the point across, by using the term "lust" when I say it is OK to "lust" after your own spouse. Yes, it's OK! It's OK to "lust" (super super passionately desire) after your own spouse. That's why God gave us these desires in the first place—to have a wonderfully joyous and exciting relationship with our spouse. So we know that lust is "unlawful" when lusting after*

34

someone or something other than what is legally or lawfully ours. But it is absolutely OK to have this same "intensity of feelings" when it is directed toward our spouse.

CHAPTER 8

Hey you single guys !

I Corinthians 7:8,9

A long time ago I too was a single guy. Well actually, it was October of 86. Yet, sometimes it seems like it was just yesterday, and sometimes it seems like it was over fifty years ago. One thing I can say is that it is imbedded in my mind like nothing else in my life. If there is one group of people today who deserve our constant prayers, it is the young Christian men of today. My brothers, "I feel your pain" as our presiding president would say. Wow, do you guys have it tough! You are living in a world and time like no other. Not since Sodom and Gomorrah has sexual perversion been so rampant and so accepted; in fact, it is even "encouraged" and "glorified" by the unsaved world. Whenever I read the papers or watch the news it just seems to be a constant barrage of pushing the sexual boundaries and norms of society to new limits. How far can we go? What will the current bear? From TV, to movies, to music, to art, it's an ever-gathering rolling stone of degradation and filth. My eyes are ever to the skies looking for the Lord's wrath. It will come, you can rest assured. But when? Only God knows!

So, considering the state in which we are forced to live and co-exist, how is a young, or an older single man for that matter, expected to survive? No sex till marriage! No self-stimulation. No lusting!

No sex till marriage: *"I say therefore to the unmarried and widows, It is good for them if they abide even as I. But if they cannot contain, let them marry: for it is better to mary than to burn" (I Corinthians 7:8-9).*

No self-stimulation: *"The wife hath not power of her own body, but the husband: and likewise also the husband hath not power of his own body, but the wife" (I Corinthians 7:4).*

No lusting: *"Lust not after her beauty in thine heart; neither let her take thee with her eyelids. For by means of a whorish woman a man is brought to a piece of bread: and the adulteress will hunt for the precious life. Can a man take fire in his bosom, and his clothes not be burned? Can one go upon hot coals, and his feet not be burned? So he that goeth in to his neighbour's wife; whosoever toucheth her shall not be innocent" Proverbs 6:25-29).*

For a single Christian man the breaking of these laws is called fornication. "It's just impossible not to do those things, to live a pure life like that", you might say. No, it's not impossible. If it were, God would not have commanded us so. And for the slip-ups, there's a thing called "Grace"! Oh thank God for His Grace and Sacrifice on the cross! For without it we would all surely burn. My friend, there is a way. It is possible to live spiritually in a sexual world. Let's start off by tackling the subject from two different angles. First, let's look at what category you might fall into. Category one: You've been a Christian all or most of your life and you've never known a world apart from God's. If you fall into this category, then you have a lot easier road ahead of you than those in the second category. If you were saved at an older age you fall into the second category, which is the category that I am in, and you have a rough road ahead. Depending on what time in your life you were saved will determine what degree of difficulty you will encounter.

Since I know it first-hand, let me give you my scenario. I was not saved until I was in my early twenties. I had many years of co-habitating with the world topped by an active and over-exposed sexual demeanor. Like the average male of the times, sex was probably the biggest part of my "psychy" and a constant topic of discussion. Changing this thought pattern a complete 180 degrees is no small feat. But by the same token, with God as your strength and your help, it is not impossible! *"God is our refuge and strength. A very present help in trouble" (Psalm 46:1).*

Let me encourage you in this point by first presenting to you a few life situations. Let's begin with this example. Let's say you are now twenty-five years old; you just got saved two years ago in the prime of your sexual hormonal explosion, and you want to live a pure life unto the Lord and wait for marriage. Let's list your obstacles and your strengths. First, expect a massive frontal attack from your number one enemy, Satan. He will hit you with all he's got! He knows your weaknesses and he knows of your desire to serve the Lord, and that's exactly where he'll attack. The last thing he wants is for you to be living a victorious life for the Lord. He wants you stopped, destroyed, broken, discouraged, and if possible, dead. He wants you to believe it's impossible to live a pure life and that you are weak and have no power over him. Oh what a liar he is! The next obstacle is the world itself: pornography, the sexual dress norms of this present culture and the never-ending frontal lobotomy of the perverted secular world. Another obstacle, you have your old friends (the Guys) who will ridicule you to scorn, in addition to your co-workers and even your unsaved family (if your family is unsaved). I remember a good friend of mine who was ostracized from his family because he wanted to wait till he was married to have sex. Their response was, "Why? What's the point?" They just didn't get it! They saw no need for it nor its relevance to the normal conduct of today's society. So as you can see, the forces against you will be great. The obstacles you will face will be staggering. Can you handle it? Or will you fold? I know I'm coming down hard, but this is not a child's game. There are many things at stake, and I feel that by exposing them all now, the better prepared for the battle you will be. So just what is at stake? My brother please hear me out. Whatever sins you commit now as a Christian man can have future negative effects later on. The choices we make, the roads we take, all have consequences. "Yes, but ah", you say, "God will always forgive and give me a second chance, right? I can have all the fun I want now and just ask for forgiveness later on." Or you might say, "I want my chance to experience life like everyone else did." Again, my friend, this is a very dangerous road you're traveling. Yes, Jesus will forgive you! And yes, He will give you a new start. This is true! The question is: What damage will have already been done? Irreversible damage!

Let's look, for example, at someone who has just committed a murder. For argument's sake, let's say he also decides to become a Christian and give his life over to the Lord. Will the Lord hear his prayers? Of course! Will the Lord completely forgive him and give him a new start? Yes, most definitely! The only problem is this new brother is still held accountable for his actions. *"For whom the Lord loveth He correcteth; even as a father the son in whom he delighteth" (Proverbs 3:12).* The Bible says he still must pay his debt to society and man's laws. He is accountable for his actions. He could ask God to not let him get caught, but do you really think God will answer that prayer? What will happen is that now as a Christian he most definitely will get caught and he'll most likely go to prison for a long time. He'll get his new start and second chance, but it will be in the place where he has placed himself. Maybe he'll lead other prisoners to the Lord, maybe he'll do and accomplish many things for the Lord; this can all be true, but unfortunately, they'll all be from behind prison bars. God will work and do mighty things in our lives but they're always effected by our circumstances. In this case, the Lord will do a work in this man's life, but it will be in the confines of God's permissive will. What the Lord had in store for him if he had not committed that crime, the man will never know. He'll never know what God's perfect will might have been for him. He'll always be loved and he'll be going to eternal glory in heaven; but still, the greater blessings will never be known.

In the realm of sexual sins and fornications there are many things to be put in the balance. For starters, there's the ever growing risk of getting some type of venereal disease; not to mention the life-threatening disease of Aids. How about your testimony for the Lord? What will the unsaved world think of your Jesus and your so-called "Born Again-ism"? In their mind, will you be just another fallen hypocritical holy roller? Think of the disgrace to your local congregation and the effect in its community. And how about your destruction of that young lady. Do you think she'll have any respect for Christianity? Will Christian men, in her eyes, now be just like any other man of this sinful world? Oh and let's not forget the possible child that might become a part of this picture. Will you support him or her? What type of life can you give this child? Think of the effect on this child's future. How will you justify your sin while trying to instill Godly values? Is this girl even a Christian? What of the plans the Lord might have had for her? I know this is all very heavy and negative—but hey, it is negative! It might be the most cataclysmic and dramatic event in your life. And that's not the

38

worst. How about the most important result to consider—your outright and premeditated sin against, not only yourself, the child, and the girl, but the premeditated sin against Your Lord! Remember what David said, "Against You and You only have I sinned".

My friend, I've known many men—Christian Men—who have fallen victim to this sin and did not wait till marriage. Has the Lord still used them? Yes, but I also know the problems they've encountered as a result of their sins of the flesh. God will not be mocked! Yes, He does still chastise and hold people accountable for their sins. Also, I believe that many of the problems in marriage, and especially the sexual aspect of it, have been a direct result of this type of sin. I often ask young men who are contemplating these acts of the flesh, "Do you have any idea of the kind of blessings you could have—not to mention the sexual pleasures—by just waiting till you're married?" Just try to imagine the precious treasure and unexpected marvel of the honeymoon night of two young people who are both virgins never knowing sex but have dedicated their bodies to the Lord. Sad to say, this phenomenon will never be experienced by most of today's young people. And you can, without a doubt, fully believe that God will reward them mightily and, yes, sexually! Yes, God did create sex and He designed it to be enjoyed to the "Max"! *"Let thy fountain be blessed: and rejoice with the wife of thy youth. Let her be as the loving hind and pleasant roe; let her breasts satisfy thee at all time, and be thou ravished always with her love"* *(Proverbs 5:18-19)*. The only condition was that it be within the confines of the marriage Bed! *"Marriage is honourable in all, and the bed undefiled: but whoremongers and adulterers God will judge"* *(Hebrews 13:4)*.

Oh, I know about all the many excuses used today to rationalize the sin of sex before marriage: "Oh, I want to make sure we're compatible. I want to make sure I really love her. Living together just makes common sense. Once you get married it ruins everything, the thrill is all gone. Once you're married there's no more sex life and life is over. If anyone finds out that I'm still a virgin I'll be laughed to scorn. I'll be the laughing stock of my friends. It's impossible in today's world to remain pure. It's unheard of." Why, I've even heard it said that it's "unhealthy". Dear brother, if any of these things where even remotely true, if any of these ideas were based on any fact, God would have said so! Who is the One who knows what we need best, the One who knows what works? Would it not be the One who has created us! Can a computer designer know the best environment for running a car's engine better than an engine builder Himself? The choice is always yours to obey or disobey. God will never twist an arm or coerce His child. Whose will will you follow? Yours or God's!

So what do you do? How do you exist in this world? Well coming to know the Lord late in your life has its drawbacks but it also has its advantages. One thing I know is this: I know what I've been delivered from! My life is a miracle in itself—being lifted out from the sexual perversions and sins to a life of serving the Lord! My friend, stay away from the old stomping grounds! Stay away from those old friends! *"Therefore if any man be in Christ, he is a new creature: old things are passed away; behold, all things are become new"* (*II Corinthians 5:17*). Find good Christian fellowship, preferably male. Try to hook up with a Brother who is a more mature Christian than yourself. Stay in The Word constantly! Pray without ceasing (keep eyes open while driving please!). And, now this is a major one, only date Christian women! I just can't stress this enough! Don't rationalize and think you're gonna turn them to the Lord. It's simply not God's will for you to date non-Christians! DON'T DO IT! Remember King Solomon? He was the wisest man to live and yet he fell because He layed with and even married non-believers. *"But King Solomon loved many strange women, together with the daughter of Pharaoh, women of the Moabites, Ammonites, Edomites, Zidonians, and Hittites; of the nations concerning which the Lord said unto the children of Israel, Ye shall not go in to them, neither shall they come in unto you: for surely they will turn away your heart after their gods: Solomon clave unto these in love"* (*I Kings 11:1-3*).

No more bar hopping and "R" movies. Anything that will stimulate you sexually will only heighten your chances of falling. I know it's not easy, but it's also not impossible! You say you love the Lord, you say you believe the Bible? Prove it! Start by reading the book of Proverbs. It deals with these problems with clear understandable advise. For the Brother who's been saved most of his life, my advise is simple. You know The Word, you know what God has done in the past and what He can do for you in the future. Remember, God is a rewarder of them who diligently seek Him. Hold fast! Don't be swayed by the adversary. Pray for that special girl to come along, and she will! God will make it happen! This is a prayer that God will definitely answer in the affirmative! If you are dating—and I don't recommend it—don't spend time alone together. Don't fall into the trap by thinking that just making out is OK and that you know when to stop. It's just not possible! Maybe one time, maybe two times, but sooner or later the flesh will overtake you. Try not to focus on your sexual future but on your spiritual future. Concentrate on all the wonders and blessings that the Lord will have in store for you and your bride-to-be. Study the Scriptures dealing with the ways of the Christian husband and what the Lord expects of you:

*Husbands, love your wives, even as Christ also loved the Church, and gave Himself for it. (**Ephesians 5:25**)*
*Husbands, love your wives, and be not bitter against them. (**Colossians 3:19**)*
*Likewise, ye husbands, dwell with them according to knowledge, giving honour unto the wife, as unto the weaker vessel, and as being heirs together of the grace of life; that your prayers be not hindered. (**I Peter 3:7**)*

*Nevertheless let every one of you in particular so love his wife even as himself; and the wife see that she reverence her husband. **(Ephesians 5:33)***

*For this cause shall a man leave his father and mother, and shall be joined unto his wife, and they two shall be one flesh. **(Ephesians 5:31)***

Speak to your pastor about your choice for a wife. Get another honest opinion of your choice. Ask yourself if you can see yourself being with this person for the rest of your eternal life; that this is it, this is and has to be the one. Most importantly, make sure this is God's will for you. Ask the Lord in prayer to give you a clear head to make the right decision. Does this woman share your dreams and desires? Does she want to serve the Lord in the same capacity that you do? Discuss different scenarios that might appear in life. Is she willing to follow you if you received the call to serve the Lord in whatever capacity? How about children? Do you share in the values and techniques that would be required in raising them? Will money be a tender issue? Will the simple things in life satisfy you both if the Lord deems it necessary for you to be in that particular state for a season? If you haven't discussed these things together then you haven't really talked. You don't really know each other. I know these are heavy questions to ask when you're in love and just want to enjoy the moment, but they are crucial if you are serious about doing God's will and living a life pleasing and glorifying to Him. The rewards can be mighty, both in this world, and in the next. One thing you can be sure of is that it's all worth it when God's will is also your's!

CHAPTER 9

To therapy or not

Psalm 73:26

Did you ever hear the story about the man who went to his therapist for help only to find that his therapist was on vacation? When he asked the receptionist how could this be when he had a scheduled appointment, the receptionist answered, "Oh, he's on a regiment of low stress and plenty of rest". "How about me?" asked the man. The receptionist responded, "'You' are the 'stress' he needs the rest from!" Oh therapy! It's become an idiom of our times. It seems everybody is going, knows someone who is going, or is thinking about going to a therapist themselves. It's a wonder how the human race ever made it all these years without it. I'm just amazed how far it's permeated our society. I mean, there's therapy for everything: from all kinds of phobias, to addictions, to whatever the market will bear! The phrase "I've got to first consult my therapist about this" has become a common escape! I think the reason why it's so appealing today is that in this "me" generation there's so much "me" that no one is listening to the other guy's problems. People are hurting, big time, out there and nobody is on the receiving end. We've become a society of transmitters without receivers. It's kind of ironic in this age of the information highway, the Internet, cellular phones, and fax machines, that no one is listening. The question I had to ask myself was, "Are things really that different than they were, say, thirty or twenty or even ten years ago? Is there really more stress and pressures and demands now than there was back during the great depression?" Well, yes and no. I know what you're saying: "Oh, another one of those cop-out answers". No, this is no cop-out but rather a type of oxymoron escape. You see, while it seems more stressful now, the truth is that back in the "Great Depression" there was plenty of reasons for stress: i.e. no jobs, no money, hungry families to feed, sickness, poverty, war, violence, crime, and plenty of uncertainty. I wonder what would happen if our present-day society had to face these trials of life. Wow! Well you can argue, "Life was more laid back and slower, it was a simpler time". Oh, really? War? Death? Food lines? Saying farewell to sons, husbands, and dads as they were swept off to war with no guarantees of their returning is to be called a simpler time? Why can't we handle it as they could? Where were the divorce lawyers, broken homes, and the therapists? Why weren't these people driven to a life of child molestation, rape, and drug dependency? I think you know what the answer is already: God, Jesus, and the family. That's who they leaned on, sought counsel, and found strength to go on. Life isn't a bowl of cherries. It's hard and self sacrificing with not too much time for yourself. You see, they understood that. They didn't expect more. And they were appreciative of the little perks that did appear now and then. That's the difference. They had hope and they knew that no matter what, they had Mom and Dad who loved them. They knew that God was on their side and this present life was not all that there was. Maybe they weren't all "Born Again" believers, but they still had the moral family fiber that held them together. They knew that sin was real. They followed the code: my wife is mine, and yours is yours. Yes, of course, there was sin and adultery, but you see, it wasn't accepted and joked about like it is in today's society. Back then, you were ashamed and you knew it was sin. If you did not fear repercussions from God, you at least feared them from society, and that was enough. I know I'm getting a little carried away, but it just disturbs me when we try to look for excuses and causes for today's problems. We let Satan convince us that through are own intelligence we can find solutions to all of our problems apart from God. Satan deviously advises "Don't seek Godly wisdom, fix it yourself." So do we really need therapy today? Yes, we do. But we shouldn't. Our so-called enlightened generation has created this dependent monolith. We've made our bed, and you know the rest. Therapy I'm afraid is here to stay, and can help, but only when the proper guidelines and standards are followed and only when it's called upon for the right reasons and circumstances. Picking a "professional friend", as I like to call them, is a serious matter. First, you have to determine what you require among all the bombastic titles. "Do I need a psychiatrist, a psychologist, a counselor, therapist, pastor, or maybe just a good friend?" Then there's the humility factor. "If I need professional help then I really have a problem, and what if my friends find out or my church? What will they think of me?" Another question is "How do I know when it's time to get help. And if I do, does that mean that I'm not trusting in the Lord for my deliverance?" These are all common questions. The answers to them all are in you. What I mean is that if you ask ten different Christians, you'd probably get ten different answers. Oh yes, the so-called theologians will battle back and forth on the dogma of doctrines and such, but in the end what matters is what and how the Lord has spoken to "you"! Only through much prayer and daily Bible study can you know the will of God for you. Remember, it's a personal relationship that you received at your conversion to Christ. A personal relationship can't exist without communication between the two parties. Take your time and don't make knee-jerk reactions. I've personally found that when important decisions have to be made and I am searching to recognize what is God's will for me, deep down inside the answer was always there. So maybe I'll get some flack from other people regarding the option I'm taking; well so be it, for it is with God that I have to do! Let God be the judge, let your spirit be the judge!

So let's start with some basic questions. "Do I need help?" Again, first seek the Lord in prayer, asking Him to guide you in the right direction. Then ask yourself these questions: "Am I getting better?" "Are other people getting hurt because of my problem?" "Is my family and church being affected?" "Am I bringing glory to God, and what of my testimony for Christ?" "Can I be an effective witness or is my problem destroying my possible service to the King?" Last, but not least is: "How long have I been struggling and not gaining any ground?" My friend, if you gave an unfavorable answer to even one of these questions, then maybe you need some mild direction. Reading this book is a start, and I hope the words spoken here can help you, and in most cases I feel it should be enough to get you on the road to Spiritual victory! Having a trusted Christian praying for you is also a good idea at this stage. If you answered unfavorably to more than three of the questions, then maybe it's time to prayerfully seek out council. So where to? Let's start by eliminating what you don't need. Number one, unless you are in prolonged depression and/or having trouble existing in society, and/or you feel that your family, friends, or yourself are in any physical danger, then you should not need a psychiatrist. Now let's discuss what you can use. The answer to this may be simpler than you think. Your choices are wide open: from a Christian psychologist, to a Christian therapist, to a Christian counselor, to your own pastor. All of these are good choices depending on your financial and logistic situation. The one imperative requirement is that they be "Born-again" believers by faith in Jesus "alone"! Under NO circumstances at all should you ever seek counsel from any unbeliever; be it friend or family. You'd be better off asking for flying lessons from a bus driver than to seek unsaved council. (Proverbs 28:5) No matter how good or cheap it is, it can never work. You are a child of God and not of this world.(II Corinthians 5:17) So the advice of this world can never do anything but drive you deeper into it. Now let's take this one step further. "What do I avoid and what do I look for?" Let's start with your pastor. This is probably the best place to start for a number of reasons. Number one being it's free. Number two, it's probably close by. And Number three, it's a familiar surrounding where you can be at ease. I found this to be the best starting point, but of course, if for some reason you feel uncomfortable or if it's unproductive, then by all means move on. So what do we have? Counselor or therapist? Basically they're both the same. One may have more academics behind him than the other, but remember, a degree on the wall doesn't always mean they know everything. You could have the most success with a mature trusted Christian friend. It's all situation specific. One of the most important things to look for is "Spiritual" counseling. If you're not being quoted scripture over and over, then something's wrong! Stay away from psychotherapy and sexual therapy. The less sex is discussed the better off you'll be. And that brings me to this point. Don't ever, ever, ever go to a female therapist or friend or whatever and start talking sex! A good example of this came from my own experience. I was going through my mid-life crises (at least I thought so). I was getting these panic attacks and getting real "bummed out" on life, and marriage, and the whole thing. So under protest I went for help. I heard from a friend that she knew a good counselor and the minute I heard the word "woman" something clicked. I thought to myself, "Hey, this might not be too bad". And when I spoke to her it sounded even better; and "forget about" when I actually saw her! Well first off she was young, she was blonde, she had a nice figure and she wanted to talk to me about my sex life. However, the minute she started asking me about how I feel about the vagina-breast relationship, I knew it was time to leave. Don't get me wrong, I'm no super Christian. I wanted to stay and talk and fantasize all day, but the Holy Spirit inside told me it was not the place for a Christian man to be and definitely not a place to receive guidance! I even asked to see her doctrinal statement and asked her about her church and walk with the Lord. She sounded right on target and she probably was; I'm not saying she wasn't a good therapist. I believe she was saved and that she helped many people; I just didn't agree with her methods and her lack of spiritual guidance. Compared to her, the next person I saw was like night and day. For starters he was a man, he was a Pastor at a local church. He was getting on in years and was full of Godly wisdom. He was also a certified Christian counselor with many years of service to the Lord and His people. The biggest shock to me was that he didn't talk about me and my mother and what I experienced as a child. He just asked a few general questions about why I was there. From that point on he did all the talking; ninety nine percent of it was from the Word of God! Scripture, Scripture, and more Scripture was all I heard mixed in with some personal testimony. Turns out he struggled with the same thing for years and was able to give excellent Godly advice. My friend, many of these "professional friends" out there are wasting people's time and money and making you do all the work. You, talking for thirty minutes about what turns you on and how bad you love women is not helping anyone but maybe your counselor and your own vocal cords. I'm not saying that in certain situations this type of therapy might not work, it can. But too much of it is being used improperly, and worst of all, unsuccessfully. Twenty, thirty, fifty, or even a hundred dollars an hour is a lot to spend to hear yourself complain about how your parents messed you all up. Getting help is good, using the help is even better. What I mean is: applying what you heard or learned is the only way all this help is going to work. I was a big one for getting some new self-help "Christian" audio tape, bragging about how profound it was, and then never applying it to my life. What's the use? Going to church each week and hearing a great message and then not using it is like eating a great steak and then spitting it out when you're done. You've enjoyed the dinner but received no nutrition! What's the point? So many Christians have strong beliefs; they know exactly what the Word of God says and can list all the doctrines of importance; but on the other hand, their daily practice of living shows no sign of their beliefs at all: "I know the Bible says so, and I believe it's true, but this is my girlfriend and I enjoy living with her", they say. Then when their world falls apart and all seems lost, they cry out to God and say, "How can you be letting this happen to me, with all I've done for You!" All of us, it seems, fall into this category at one time or another. We blame the Lord whenever something's gone wrong; and then totally forget Him when everything is going great. But, thank God for His Mighty Grace, He just keeps on forgiving and loving and giving new starts! The thing we must remember is that, though He gives new starts, we still bear the consequences of our blunders. He just takes us at that point and starts us out anew.

My friend, getting help is good and can really help at times. The point we all have to come to is "application" and "more application". We will never move from point A to point B if we don't put into practice what we've learned. I know sometimes we're like "old dogs" and need the same lesson over and over again. But until that moment in time when we allow the Word to overcome the flesh, we will never ever recover from what we've become. Seek Godly help! Desire to change! Pray for victory! And "continually" seek God's wisdom through prayer and daily Bible reading and study. To listen is noble; to apply it is divine!

CHAPTER 10

Daddies, don't let your sons grow up to be "girl watchers" —

Proverbs 29:17

I remember back when I was about twelve or thirteen, we used to hang out and play like the rest of "kiddum". Having those long "un-intellectual" conversations with my buddies about "the future" was a common nightly ritual. I distinctly remember saying, "When I have kids I'm going to be the 'koolest' dad around; my kids will be able to do anything they want." Wow! Do those words ever come back to haunt me every now and then. The mind of a child and an adult are — or I should say "should be" — miles apart. What seemed so important, so earth shattering, and so life shaking as a child, now seems ridiculous and completely illogical. I remember back when I was in high school I was kind of a head "rock-n-roller wanna be" and being "kool" was the most crucial point of my existence. To be "kool" was to be liked, and to be liked was to fit in. Fitting in was the first step to "acceptancy", and not to drag this out longer than necessary, "acceptancy" meant being someone you were not. I remember this one time in particular, I was being my long-haired self and found myself attracted to this young girl named Mary. Mary was, in school-house logistics, as far from my persona type as New York is from LA. Mary was a dear sweet girl. She was highly intelligent and in all Honors Classes. She was a plain girl, thin and fair skinned. She had lovely big brown eyes. She was definitely not at all one of the "in crowd" "trendy" people, but fit in more I guess with the smart "nerdy" group. She had a plain face and a plain figure, and to my best recollection never had a boyfriend before me (I surmised this by the fact that she didn't know how to kiss, like I did). Never-the-less, she liked me and I her. There was only one problem. We could not be seen together at school because, well, she was not acceptable "babe material". And to be fair, I would not have been considered appropriate male companionship in the eyes of her friends, nor her mother. The thing that got me was the fact that she really liked me. She would buy me the sweetest gifts which I was embarrassed to receive. She desired sweet innocent romance and I desired to grab what ever I could. She always refused, God bless her. Even though I thought mainly with my "pubescent" hormonal brain, I really liked her and wanted to date her. She really would have been good for me. I guess you know what happened. Yes, even though she was not offended by my disassociation of her in public, I broke up with her. You know, I haven't thought about her until now and I'm getting a strange sense of sadness for those foolish acts and the wonder of what might have been. See what I mean about irrational behavior. Is there any sense in that at all?

No! But I was behaving the only way I knew how. Yes, you could say it was part peer pressure; but why do some kids respond to peer pressure one way and some the other? Why did I have to look "kool"? Why should she have been considered unacceptable merely because she was not a "sex kitten wild girl"? And why, oh why, did I feel that being with her sexually had to be? How about my respect for her as a person, a women (to be)? Why, to my mind, was she just supposed to be a "sex object", and those good feelings for her to be suppressed? Could it be hereditary? Could it be that I learned them from my father? Or could it be that I was just a guy having fun and falling prey to my ever-evolving animal urges?

This generation seems to be a generation of "Not me", "It's not my fault". Nobody's willing to be held personally accountable for anything. Blaming one's dysfunctional family is common place and is considered acceptable cause for irrational behavior. I totally disagree, and I don't want to be accused of one who shares that belief! So when I speak on the "sins of the father", I don't want to be accused of being one of those "My-Daddy-made-me-do-it" people. So let me begin by addressing the excuse, "My Daddy made me do it". Well, he did and didn't. Now what do I mean by that? The Bible speaks of the sins of the father being passed down from generation to generation in Exodus 20:5 *"Thou shalt not bow down thyself to them, nor serve them: for I the Lord thy God am a jealous God, visiting the iniquity of the fathers upon the children unto the third and fourth generation of them that hate me."* The Bible also says a lot about raising children and the accountability that parents have. When the Bible says in Proverbs 22:6 to *"Train up a child in the way he should go: and when he is old, he will not depart from it",* does that also go the other way? If we train up a child in the best way we know how, and that way is a way of evil and sin, will that child not depart from it? Will he or she continue that lifestyle of sin? I think the evidence demands an overwhelming "Yes". Yes, our children will carry our attitudes, our prejudices, and all of our hang-ups. This is not to say that it's all written in stone, but — barring conversion to Christ — it's safe to say that "The apple doesn't fall far from the tree". Thinking back to when I was growing up, I now can see that watching and mimicking one's parents is not something that you do intentionally, but rather, subconsciously. I knew my dad disliked blacks, so I disliked blacks. I knew he disliked Jews, so I disliked them. And when it came to sex and the "manly" thing to do, well my dad read *"Playboy",* so I read it too. When a shapely girl would walk by or was shown on TV I knew his responses and I mimicked them. Now my Dad never came out and said, "Hey, some women are for marrying and some are sex objects to lust after", but I knew that's how he felt. Porn books, X-rated movies, topless joints and "girl watching" were what I experienced, so that's what I did. I knew that sex was not only for marriage (or so I thought) because my Dad gave me my first condom and told me to have fun, but be careful! Why, I even remember the time I had my first sexual encounter and the pride I felt; I couldn't wait to tell my dad! Hey, even my mother knew and just accepted it as "boys being boys". I wonder if that girl's parents would have felt the same way about it? But then again, this is the nineties and, unfortunately, the girls-just-want-to-have-fun" theme runs just as rampant. Again, I don't want to discredit my parents and accuse them of premeditated "unparenting" (they loved me dearly and would do anything to see me happy and successful) but all they themselves could go by was what their parents told them, and what they saw their own parents do. And when the rest of the world is doing it the same way, it makes one feel that, surely ,it must be OK. My parents are now saved and living whole-heartily for the Lord and I know they're forgiven, just as I am. The fact still remains that I let in evil (into my mind and my being) through the "eye gate " and it is forever there. The thoughts and visions from all that pornography will always be there. It's a fact of life, and Satan knows it too and will use that weakness whenever he can. And he will do the same in our son's (or future sons) lives to bring them down.

So what do we do? How do we shield our children from this filth and prepare them for what lies ahead? It would be nice to lock them in a room and only let them out when they are twenty one. Of course we know that's impossible and would still not prepare them to avoid the evils that this "fallen world" has to offer. I feel the one, most important, thing to remember is this: Everything that our children let in — every TV commercial to which they are exposed, every movie they watch, and all that they hear from their friends — it is all permanent! Once anything is let in, it's in forever. If it's good material, then praise God! But if it's evil, it's with them for the rest of their lives. And worst of all is that our minds have a tendency to "focus" on the evil and "block out" the good. So watch out! Simply, don't let your children be exposed to anything that you would not feel comfortable showing to Jesus Himself. If that might mean no TV, then by God do it! I know what you're already thinking, and I've heard it a million times before; but Yes, I'm saying, shield your children from the world — the evils of it! Why is that so hard to understand? Satan has tricked us again. He tells us, "Oh, your children will be unbalanced. They will be naive to the world, and won't be individuals". So what Satan is really saying is that we should expose our children to whatever they want, whatever the world has to offer, tell them "just do it" and let them make their own decisions. Seems to me, that's exactly what the world is doing now, and look at the great results they've been having: unprecedented violence, sex from ten years old and up, crime, drugs, abortions, teenage suicide; and it's getting worse every single day. Do you think we've been duped? Oh yeah! We've been duped big time! Lets start "unduping" ourselves by getting rid of the hypocrisy in our own lives. If we say we know what is right and good, then let's live it. Shut down the TV, cut out the secular music, or at least screen it, for Heavens sake! And by all means, "NO Music TV"! If any one thing has sped up the decay of our society, it has been

Music TV. Twenty-four hours a day, seven days a week — sex, violence, sex-violence, total blasphemy, disrespect for parents and all authority — all day, all the time! Well at least they have their individuality (in sarcasm): baggy pants, oversized clothes and an earring in every part of their body. If they're looking to be different and make a statement; hey, why not try Jesus! Parents, stop listening to the psychologists and politicians and the so-called authorities on child behavior and listen to God! The world has given these people and their theories a chance and the results are quite obvious: "It doesn't work!" I don't care how out of date it sounds; live a life pleasing to the Lord and society will change — no sex before marriage, respect for the body that God gave you, respect for women as equals, treating women as one of the important ingredients to God's recipe for a harmonious society. If it takes a sacrifice on our part, then so be it. Are not our children worth it? I'm just amazed at what I hear out there in the, "real world". I was talking to this one fella who was proclaiming how his children were the most important thing to him. He was saying this because he was determined that his ex-wife's live-in boyfriend had to live up to his standards, because, as he put it, "I want my kids to have a safe environment to live in". Now his statement just begs the question: Hey, if they were that important to you, then why didn't you just stay together with your wife and family? He claimed his wife and he just "fell out of love after ten years of marriage. Hey, if they were really that important to him, he could have stayed together with his wife. But that would have meant personal sacrifice, an option very rarely pursued in this day and age. We have to break the cycle! We have to mold our children right from the get-go. If we start the moment they can crawl, then they won't know any other way. If your children are already teenagers, then tell them you were wrong; explain what the Bible says and reflect back on your own mistakes. Tell them you know you can't make them do anything, but that you hope they will think about and ponder your advice. Tell them you love them, that you'll stand by them, but that you also feel very strongly about your beliefs and you'll never condone or approve of their actions apart from God's Word. It's not easy, and the older they are the harder it will be. There are no "guarantees" that our children will grow to love and serve the Lord. Because God is a loving and gracious God, He has given us all "free will" to believe or not to believe. This is true also of our children, they are not born Christians. They're born with an old sin nature just like us. All we can do is show them "The Way" — belief in Jesus as their own personal Savior — read them the Word, and pray without ceasing. We are bound by the Scriptures to train them in the ways of God. The younger they are when you start, the better. And yes, drill it into them soon! You only have a short time. They say that a child's personality is already partially formed by the time he's five years old. But it's never too late! Dads, please hug your wives in the presence of your children. Show them you have respect for your wife and that you love her. Tell them and show them your devotion, first and foremost, to God; and secondly to your family, placing yourself last. If you want them to go to church, then you go also. If you expect them to live a holy life, then you abide also. The phrase "actions speak louder than words" is all so true! Apply it and live by it! Be that Godly example! Tell your children of God's love for them and of His mighty plans for each and every one of us. Tell them of the reward of waiting for marriage and remaining pure. Explain to them that you understand how difficult it is and of the opposition they may (will) encounter. Tell them it's worth the cost. Tell them of how God has worked mightily in your own life, and how also you paid the price and endured the chastisement of God for following the flesh. Explain to them the world and its ways and how doing the right thing isn't always the easy thing. Pray with them, pray for them! Let them know how you were hurt and betrayed by this world. Tell them that you understand their desire to experience what's out there and tell them that a mistake made now can be unfixable even by you. If they want true happiness and joy and peace, it's "only" found in Christ! You can bet Satan will be doing his part to pull them toward himself. He has them ninety percent of the time (at school, with their friends, watching TV, etc) so you better make very sure that "your" ten percent is "good"! When they are at home, make sure that you devote that time to them and to your family. After all, it is the only time that you have to demonstrate to them your devotion to God and your devotion to them. You certainly can't do it when they are in school, or outside playing with their friends, or when they are in bed sleeping. So when they are at home, change your habits, instead of vegetating in front of the TV, spend that time talking and playing with them. Make that time "count" with your family. And make sure some of that time is set aside as an actual time of Bible study and prayer. Teach them how to pray by allowing them to hear you pray. Share with them the favorite verses that Jesus has shown to you in His Word so that they may also benefit and grow in Christ. It does not have to be a long Bible study. A few minutes (maybe at the dinner table) can be priceless!

Dads, there is also another part of this training that we all try to avoid and usually fail miserably at: that's in the area of sex education. For starters, throw out all the literature you have of the world's. The world has nothing to offer but confusion and alternatives, which are not alternatives. Let's start with dating. I could give you my opinion but I'd rather have the Lord say it. *I Corinthians 7:1,2,9* *"Now concerning the things whereof ye wrote unto me: It is good for a man not to touch a woman. Nevertheless, to avoid fornication, let every man have his own wife, and let every woman have her own husband. But if they cannot contain, let them marry: for it is better to marry than to burn."* Dating is out! Yes, you heard me. Out! If they want to have friends, fine. If they want to have a party under your supervision, fine also; but as for dating, no way! If you search the Scriptures you'll not find dating anywhere. The person that you, so-called, dated or courted (or whatever), was the one you planned to marry. That doesn't mean that you had to marry that person, but that you had plans to and that was the only reason for the courting. Pretty impossible you say? With men, maybe; but with God, you know the rest. ***Matthew 19:26*** *"But Jesus beheld them, and said unto them, With men this is impossible; but with God all things are possible."* One of the greatest tools for child rearing is "play at your house". Make all attempts to make your home the place where everybody wants to hang out. Put up a basketball hoop, do whatever. Make your child's friends feel welcomed and unjudged. You might have to put up with a little craziness and loud music, but you'll always know Where your children are, Who they are with, and What they are doing — three important W's in child rearing. Be the "kool" parent and try to include your children's friends in all of your activities. Don't push your beliefs but rather demonstrate them by your actions of love and concern, unconditionally. You'd be amazed at how far this will go. The best thing you can achieve is an environment where you kids' friends are coming to you for advice, and don't be surprised if your own kids feel uncomfortable with this little arrangement. Tough! Now some controversial "Don'ts". Don't approve of or suggest masturbation as a form of hormone embattlement. I know this is a scary area and everybody's afraid to ask their pastor. So I did it for you. It is wrong and forbidden in the Bible. It's that simple — for male or female! I Corinthians 7:4 tells us your body belongs to your future mate, *"The wife hath not power of her own body, but the husband: and likewise also the husband hath not power of his own body, but the wife."* When dealing with your son or daughter, one thing not to do is to make an issue out of it. And by all means, don't walk in and say to your teen "Are you masturbating?" The wall will go up and might never come down. Another thing, please, if you ever catch them, please don't make a scene. Shut the door and wait about a month before you even think of bringing it up. Now psychologists might tell you it's good and natural, but it's not! It only formulates fantasies and lust, and in time, can become an out-of-control addiction. Tell them their body is not their own, and it should be saved for their future spouse alone. I Corinthians 7:2-4 tells us *"Nevertheless, to avoid fornication, let every man have his own wife, and let every woman have her own husband. Let the husband render unto the wife due benevolence: and likewise also the wife unto the husband. The wife hath not power of her own body, but the husband; and likewise also the husband hath not power of his own body, but the wife."* Another thing, forget about safe sex and condoms — there is no such thing as "safe sex"! And most importantly, it is fornication — a sin! It's against themselves, it's against their sexual partner, and most of all, it's against God! I Corinthians 6:18-20 tell us to *"Flee fornication. Every sin that a man doeth is without the body; but he that committeth fornication sinneth against his own body. What? Know ye not that your body is the temple of the Holy Ghost which is in you, which ye have of God, and ye are not your own? For ye are bought with a price: therefore glorify God in your body, and in your spirit, which are God's."* So there you have it, God tells us straight out that our body belongs to Him — He purchased it with His own blood — and using our body in fornication is a sin against Him!   Another "don't" is don't look at pornography; don't read it, don't tempt it, don't even think about it. It's like a cancer that drains you of everything you are, and leaves you weak and helpless to fight off its power.   The Bible tells us to be on our guard against becoming helpless, and also how to combat being helpless.   Romans 12:21 counsels, *"Be not overcome of evil, but overcome evil with good."* Don't take into yourself, though the eyegate, any self-destructive material; but rather, saturate yourself with the things of God — read your Bible and get to know Him! Proverbs 25:28 warns us that *"He that hath no rule over his own spirit is like a city that is broken down, and without walls. **Romans 8:6** "For to be carnally minded is death; but to be spiritually minded is life and peace."*   It is very important for us Dads to protect our sons from becoming entangled in the snare of pornography. In fact, it is very important for us Dads to instill in the minds of our young boys a virtuous and Spirit-filled attitude toward how men <u>should</u> view women.   And remember, when discussing the issue of sex with your children, always be positive; don't always emphasize the negative. Tell them of all the good that awaits them for doing the right thing. If they want to know about sex, tell them of how "unbelievable" it will be when God is blessing it and sanctifying it! Yes, God did create it and He intended it to be "awesome" — but only within the confines of the "marriage bed" between a man and his wife. If we were to name a creation of God's that mankind has thoroughly corrupted, it would have to be sex. Oh how man has destroyed something that once was so beautiful!

So Dads, what's it going to be? The future of this world really rests on what man chooses to do. I know it's hard, but you must count the cost to your family, to your church, and to your own testimony to the world. Tell your boys, and yes, girls too! Tell them of the wondrous love God has for them. Tell them they are of worth, and they are significant, and they do have a purpose. Don't let your children be hooked into this secular socialist absurdity that tries to tell us that we are just animals here by some freak of cosmoses nature. God tells us straight out that we are His creation, *Genesis 1:27, "So God created man in His own image, in the image of God created He him; male and female created He them."* Don't let your children be cheated out; make sure they "know" that we are made in the image of God and we <u>can</u> make a difference. I'm tired of all the so-called intelligencea of today trying to sell to us as "fact" their theories of where we came from and what we are. Were they there? They can't even figure out who shot JFK and they are now trying to tell us that they know what happened five billion years ago and they expect us to buy it hook, line, and sinker. Dads, cut out the trash TV, pull the plug on that Internet line from hell. I was watching a special one night on the computer world and how our kids know more than the parents about their computers.   They interviewed some parents who were bewildered about what to do about their children's access to the Internet. Their biggest dilemma was that no matter what blocking device or lock they tried to implement on their PC, their kids figured it out or by-passed it. They asked "What can we do"? I couldn't believe they never even thought about or considered simply pulling the plug, cancel the service — please show me some intelligence here! There's so much we can do that's so easy. It's all common Christian sense. Cut out the trash in your own life and the children will follow suit. I'm just amazed how my own two boys mimic all that I do and say (whether it be good or bad). Our children will be just like us, and they'll raise their own kids and treat their own spouses in the same manner that we are raising them and are treating our spouse. It's all a simple equation: society today and its great fall is all a direct result of "No God", "No Dad", "No family", "No love", and "No discipline". I know, I've said it before, but it's just so obvious that it goes beyond all reasoning. The minute Jesus became just another dirty word was the minute this world began its fall. Dad, take back your position of spiritual leader, of the source of sound wisdom, and of the loving caring husband God intended you to be. In Proverbs 29:17 God instructs us to *"Correct thy son, and he shall give thee rest; yea, he shall give delight unto thy soul."* You've heard the term "no pain, no gain"; it's going to take sacrifice and effort and your only reward might be, "Thanks Dad, I love you". Won't that be enough!

CHAPTER 11

Beware the tempter's snare!

Proverbs 6:25,29

When the Bible says "Behold, all becomes new", it's not kidding! The life I now live, in the Spirit as a child of God, is so alien to the previous one. So many things have changed, not overnight mind you, but through the slow and sometimes painful hand of God. I think the first time I knew something was different in my life was the first time (after my conversion) that I was faced with receiving too much change back from a cashier. I remember being angry at myself and fighting the inner battle that only a Christian can understand. As I slowly walked towards the automatic doors I felt as if all of humanity was aware of my evil; and I wouldn't have been surprised to see news cameras waiting outside as the police cuffed and shuffled me away. I know it might sound childish to the world, but to those who have believed, it's all too real. Now this might seem like a trivial event, but the Lord works in this way to gently mold us into the Christ-like figure we will someday be. Sometimes it's the testing of the Lord, or it can be the tempting of the Devil. One thing we must remember is the difference between the two. God does not tempt us, only Satan does. "What's the difference", you might ask? Well the answer is simple. The Devil's temptations are for the sole purpose of causing you to sin, and in so doing, destroying your testimony to the world, and numbing your fellowship with Christ. When God allows trials into our life, it's only for our benefit, not to our demise. Through trials and testing we grow stronger and closer to our Lord. God knows best for each of us just how much we need and can bear, and at just the perfect time. Simply put, God deals with us in love and Satan deals with us in destruction and hate. The more mature you become as a Christian, the easier it will become to distinguish between the two. A discerning heart only comes through a close walk with the Lord and an intense study of His Word. Once you master this skill you will know what to do when faced with temptation and how to react when going through a trial. If you mislabel and treat temptations as trials, or visa versa, you will be in for a Christian life filled with grief and failure.

I had a friend years back whom I admired deeply. In this world of sex, and well, more "sex", he was able to maintain purity. He was a very handsome young man with a good build and a profession that exposed him to many, should I say, uninhibited young women. I was always impressed with his ability to stand up to the sexual attacks of Satan. There would always be some scantily-clad woman trying to hit on him. Again, his place of employment did not help at all and probably wasn't the best place for a young Christian man to be working, but as they say "that's life". The reason I bring this person up is: number one, I felt the Lord had him in my life to encourage me in my battle for righteousness. He was always a testimony to me by his love for the Lord and his ability to wait for the perfect one whom the Lord would send. In this era of premarital sex and promiscuousness, he was truly a diamond amongst the dirt. The second thing I learned from my friend and his experiences was how far Satan would go and how the Lord would only permit him to go so far. He told me of one time in particular where a young lady knew he was a Christian and could not believe he could be so good looking and not be seduced. She tried over and over, pushing this to the limits. But like Joseph's temptress, she failed. The details would not be proper for a Christian book, so I'll leave them out. What I learned from this is that the Lord knew how much temptation one person could bare, and how little it would take to destroy another. Do I think I would have stayed the course? I don't know and I'm glad back then it was not me. The Lord knew my friend was ready and maybe another man might not have been. Satan is strong, oh yes. But, praise God, our Lord is stronger!

Remember now, in all these situations the Lord is not "tempting", but is "allowing" it. He knows our greater work and future. Psalm 37:24 He will not let us, who are weak, go too far into the fire. Psalm 9:9 He will graciously work with us, over and over again, until we get it right. Yet, if you continue to succumb to it for too long, He just might let you get a little "skin burn". If you fail over and over to heed His warnings He will not forsake you; but, He might have to let you get a touch of that fire that you long for so much. Does He stop loving you? Never! He can't and He won't! Will He get you out of your predicament? He can, but He probably won't. You've heard the old adage, "You made your bed, so now lie in it"? Well you might have to lie in that bed, ironically, of your destruction. Remember, the sins we commit don't only affect us, they have grave consequences that sometimes fester into mighty saws. People get hurt, lives get destroyed, and with this world of VD (AIDS) you might even die. Yes, the Lord can pick up the pieces and start you anew, but only "from" the point you've fallen to. That means starting with all your problems and predicaments you've put yourself into. Is it worth it? By the way, this friend of mine did hold out and waited for the Lord's will, amongst the mocking and ridicule he endured; not for a week, nor a month, but for years. I'm happy to say the Lord gave him the "Girl of his dreams", a beautiful women who loves the Lord and who was also waiting for the moving of the Lord's hand. Praise God!

What does all this mean? It means: Don't think you're so strong that you can handle anything or anyone. Satan just loves to see us fall, and to present raving accusations against us. You see, every time we fail we not only disappoint God, we destroy our testimony; and in so doing, we make it that much more difficult for someone who's searching, to turn to the Lord for salvation. You know,

"Another one of those hypocritical Bible thumpers", is what they'll label you. Don't be a statistic!

When we humble ourselves to the point where we can admit we are weak and vulnerable, then we can start to allow God to plot our course, avoiding the potholes and detours of life. With our spiritual blinders on, we can shut out the smut and the flirting, and look only upwards. If you think you can play with the fire and go out to the bars and the clubs and hang out with the girls around the water cooler, you're dead wrong! The Bible doesn't say just avoid intercourse and you'll be fine. No, it says *avoid all "appearance" of evil* **Proverbs 13:21** So don't even give heed to the dirty jokes and the "innocent" innuendoes; avoid it like it was the plague! Will you be ridiculed? You can count on it! Will the Lord carry you through? You can count on that too.

It's nice to think sometimes that you coined your own phrase; but unfortunately, the odds are that you probably didn't. Someone has already been there and done that. I'd like to make my claim to fame with the catch phrase, "premeditated sin", that I used in an earlier chapter. We've all heard of premeditated murder which we know means: a thought-out predetermined plan to kill someone. You knew your target, you knew where to be and what you wanted to do. The term "accident" cannot be used, even though it's probably the first line of defense you would use to explain the bloody body on the floor. Not unlike premeditated murder, premeditated sin is often committed without weighing the cost and not thinking with a sound mind. The devil doesn't always make you do it; and saying she made me, only works in kindergarten. Premeditated sin is just that: a predetermined desire to perform an act in full knowledge that it is wrong and against our God. You're saying, "I know there's a God, I know what I'm about to do is a sin, but I just don't care". When we're in this frame of mind, many things come shining through. Number one being a total desire for self pleasure: "I need this, I worked for it, and I'm going to do it". The last thing you are willing to do is think about the consequences, so you don't. I've found that in areas of lust, premeditated sin often plays a role. It's like a bear looking at a piece of meat in a bear trap and thinking, "Hey, I know that if I take that meat it'll sure taste good, but I most likely will loose my paw or even die". And then saying, "What the heck, I'm hungry, nobody's feeding me, so I'm gonna go for it. I'll just try not to get caught." The major difference, obviously, is that a bear can't rationalize. The ironic thing is: we "can" and we "don't". You've heard the excuse, "There's a force far greater than me in control"? Well, I've been there and tried that excuse, and you know what? It's not going to cut it with God. What does the Word say? "Greater is He that is in you than he that is in the world". Don't let Satan trick you into thinking that you're too weak to fight!

Let's look into some scenarios that we've all probably experienced, like you know that on Tuesdays there's a real "looker" working at the coffee shop, so you make it your business to always stop at that particular coffee shop every Tuesday, and maybe you dress a little better that day. And maybe you like the way she flirts with you, so you flirt a little back. "There's no harm or anyone hurt", you convince yourself. But what happens? You become involved in a subconscious act of adultery without even realizing it. What happens to your testimony? Are you faithfully standing firm for the Gospel? And what if someone one day desires to hear about salvation and they ask you in front of this little "looker" you've been tempting fate with. Will you be so bold as to stand up and speak the words of Christ? Or will you slump down and slither into the shadows when confronted in front of your unsaved worldly one? Many things can be compromised when our sin becomes our driving force. Do you boldly state your love for your wife and family? And if you're single, do you proclaim with pride your desire to hold off on sex till marriage? Or does the peer pressure from the world crush you into useless grains of sand blown into obscurity by the winds of personal pride? My friend please remember, I understand these pressures and I know, firsthand, how difficult it can be in this sin-sick world. But that doesn't change the fact that it's wrong. I remember back when I would have to pick up parts at a certain part's house. I knew that in this particular one, the bathroom was filled with pornographic material. It was "always" a battle for me. It was so easy to just say I had to use the bathroom and take a quick peek. "Who would know or even care?" I would be lying if I said I never looked, even once. And I would also be lying if I didn't tell of the sin sickness and guilt I felt after the flesh gave way to sin—like being hit over the head with a baseball bat. In time, God got through and the victory was mine. Whether it's taking a fast peek at the well-endowed waitress, or flirting with the bank teller, it's all going to "get you" in the long haul. My friend, the results are always: No peace, no peace, no peace! You will never be happy! I don't care if she promises you the life of Hue Heffner, it's going to leave you wanting. Like I've said before, the scariest encounter the Lord allowed me was when He showed me that I wouldn't say "No". I always thought that I could just warm my hands on the coals and, when push came to shove, I'd say, "Sorry, I'm spoken for" and run like the wind. I was so sure of myself that the Lord put me to the test. I realized through a unique situation that the Lord allowed, that I wouldn't run. That scared the daylights out of me! Thankfully, God stopped it before it was too late and gave me the opportunity to learn a valuable lesson—never to be forgotten! As the commercial goes, "Don't try this at home".

James 1:12 I Corinthians 10:13   Always be aware of the deceiver and his ways! If Satan knows that your weakness and downfall is an open porno magazine, then you'll find them at every turn. Whatever your vice, he has his hands on the screw.

CHAPTER 12

Dressed to kill (A CRITIQUE ON MODERN SOCIETY)

II Timothy 3:1-5

Here we go again, but I guess it's all par for the course. You see, it upsets me that I have to go through all these apologetics every time I have to discuss a subject that involves some group of people of which it is not "politically correct" to discuss in the manner in which I will discuss them. What this all boils down to in simple terms is if you're not a Christian with the "Mind of Christ" dwelling in you, then what I'm about to say will appear to be discriminatory towards women. But again, because we live in this upside-down, right-is-left world, some will take this the wrong way. To save time and paper (see I'm saving a tree for the environmentalist) I'll bypass the apologies and explanations and get right to the point (please refer to chapter 7 for a detailed explanation). Though what I'm about to discuss will appear so radical that it might even border on the insane to the unsaved, and maybe even to a few Christians, it is never-the-less not my opinion, but God's. You can take two roads at this point and declare that all that God has declared in His Word is irrelevant, out-dated, ridiculous, absurd, and of no significance to this present age; or you can believe it, accept it, apply it, and live it. Again, if arms are to be taken up, take them up with The Lord God Almighty.

So where do I begin? I guess the best place is always at the beginning and for us Christians that always means "Genesis". The Creation is one of my favorite topics of discussion and always brings me into a state of awe! Right from the first moving of God's hand you can plainly see a thought-out, strategized plan. This was no "bang" of random confusion, no process of evolutionary happenstance. No, this was the mighty hand of the Lord God Almighty plotting out and directing every molecule to its slated destination. What makes this creation so unique is its order and its foresight. Most of all is the obvious signs of compassion, which evolution could never produce. Everywhere we turn we see order and a system of absolutes in which all our laws of nature must adhere to. There is beginning and there is completion. Why I'm stressing this is to expose the point that without belief in "Divine creation" you cannot apply or understand God's plan and purpose for a woman and a man. In fact, it takes more blind faith to believe in evolution and a chance happening than it would ever take to believe in a Creator. From the animal kingdom to the plant kingdom the results are obvious to the sane mind. It doesn't matter where you look, God is evident in it.

Even take sex (since this is a book about sex) I feel God is rarely given credit for it; and if anything, He's blamed for not letting us enjoy it in peace. This could not be further from the truth. We can find the work of the Lord in every aspect of it. Even take procreation itself, though I've never heard anyone discuss it, personally I find it quite fascinating. Take the female anatomy and its design. It's plain to see it was designed to accept the male genitalia perfectly. The term "fits like a glove" could not be more appropriate. I could go on and on. There's just so much if you just sit down and think about it. The breasts and their ability to produce the perfect food for a growing child. To this day they still can't reproduce this cornucopia of nutrition found only in mother's milk. And you want to discuss the unbelievable, just fathom the forming and eventual birth of a child! *"As thou knowest not what is the way of the spirit, nor how the bones do grow in the womb of her that is with child; even so thou knowest not the works of God who maketh all" (Ecclesiastes 11:5).* Yes, I know, they tell us that the animals do it the same way and in so doing make us no more than animals ourselves. This seems to be the constant tactic of the propaganda of the Darwinists and anti-creationists: to distract from the obvious and focus on the irrelevant. No matter what, everything in nature points to ordered creation, and I don't care about the monkeys. Some more food for thought is the fact that no other "animal" procreates facing its mate. (In sarcasm: I guess we just evolved a little faster). The reason I'm going through this again is to make the point clear: God has order, God has a plan, and in order for anything to work, His rules must be applied.

Now let's take a look in the Scriptures and hear from God Himself just exactly how He did, in fact, create us.

And God said, Let us make man in our image, after our likeness; and let them have dominion over the fish of the sea, and over the fowl of the air, and over the cattle, and over all the earth, and over every creeping thing that creepeth upon the earth. So God created man in His own image, in the image of God created He him; male and female created He them. (Genesis 1:26-27)

And the Lord God formed man of the dust of the ground, and breathed into his nostrils the breath of life: and man became a living soul. (Genesis 2:7)

And the rib, which the Lord God had taken from man, made He a woman, and brought her unto the man. And Adam said, This is now bone of my bones, and flesh of my flesh: she shall be called woman, because she was taken out of man. Therefore shall a man leave his father and his mother, and shall cleave unto his wife: and they shall be one flesh. And

they were both naked, the man and his wife, and were not ashamed.
(Genesis 2:22-24)

When the Lord created Adam and Eve he created more than just a male and female; besides the "physical" differences there are major emotional and psychological character traits that are unique to each. God being the Creator, "inventor" if you will, knew what each needed and didn't need, what would fortify and what would destroy. So many times we hear Christians referring to the Bible as "our owner's manual" and it's a very good analogy. In the Bible, God plainly says, do this and thrive, do that and be destroyed. So for a case in point, let's look at the male of His creation. We should all know what's good for us. We all need physical food and spiritual food. We need to be saved. We need fellowship with other believers. We need daily devotional and praise time with the Lord. We need to pray and seek God's will. We need to evangelize and proclaim the Gospel to a lost and dying world. The Bible speaks clearly of the "fruits of the Spirit" that are ours when we are "in fellowship" with our Lord and Saviour! Yes, when we put our trust in Christ the Bible says we will have peace and dwell in the house of the Lord forever! Sounds so simple, doesn't it? And these are the same guidelines that God commands for a woman. Where it changes is when we start dealing with what will "destroy" a male, and what will harm a woman. I want to go into this point in depth, but I also want to discuss why these "don't do's" are being over done, why the male seems to be targeted more than the woman, and of course, who's doing the targeting.

Let's go back to the "Divine Institutions of God", one of which is "the family". And keep in mind that God has established these institutions as guidelines and blessings for the regenerate and unregenerate alike. To have stability and order in a society, the Divine Institution of the family, the family unit, must be kept intact. So guess what was one of the first things that Satan targets for his attack: the man, the father, the dad. Destroy him, and in time, the rest will follow. One thing that a lot of Christians overlook is the fact that Satan can read the Bible as well as you or I; and by reading it, he knows our weaknesses. What does the Bible say is the male's main weakness? I hope by now you know the answer: the lust of the flesh and the weakness towards a seductive women. Satan knows this and has been attacking it ever so slowly, yet with dogged diligence. Distraction is the key that Satan uses for success in this area. Entice a man to look, and then he will lust; get him to lust, and sin lieth at the door—fornication and adultery. It didn't happen overnight, it wasn't just one look, it's been years of wearing away at the moors of society. What was once labeled pornography is now considered "art" and can even be found on prime time TV. What once would have been considered totally unacceptable is now happily embraced as good and right. Look, for example, at the fashion industry; the dress and look of today can be described as nothing less than "harlots on parade". On a recent jaunt to the shopping mall I could not get over the attire and attitude of all the young ladies and girls. With them wearing the tightest clothes and the shortest skirts, and plenty of flesh flowing, it's extremely hard to keep one's eyes looking straight ahead. Now I'm sure not all of these young ladies understand what they're portraying, and if they did, they probably wouldn't even view it as wrong. But in actuality, what their attire—rather their lack of it—is saying is "You want me, you need me, you gotta have me; and well maybe I'll give it to you". There is no area of popular culture where this is not portrayed. And it's absolutely impossible to avoid, it's everywhere. We are bombarded with it. With sex as the major advertising promotional tool, it's no wonder why there's so much rape, incest, and sex-related crimes. It even works in the church; you want to get people's attention, just mention fornication and lust and the pews come alive. Being a people without moral parents and spiritual leaders, we've become a "sin less" society meaning that people consider that nothing is wrong if everyone says it's right.

Now please do not misunderstand me. I'm not blaming sexy women for distorting men, and I am not saying that they're asking for it, Goodness no! What I am saying is that "sex-sighted" men become unfaithful husbands, absentee fathers, and followers, instead of leaders. In a world where women are "dressed to kill" and men are hungry predators, you're bound to create a self-centered, irresponsible, uncontrollable, ungodly and self-destroying example of a family leader; and in turn a deteriorated and vulnerable family unit, vulnerable to the further attacks of Satan on all of its members. I guess today people misguidedly just call it an "alternative lifestyle". What messages are we giving to our daughters and sons? Is sex all there is that matters? Do looks and dress supersede honor and character? Are we unconsciously training them to rationalize by asking such questions as: "Is looking good wrong?" or "How about beauty, is it not a creation of God?" At a "home-schooling" convention that I recently attended, I found myself in the presence of some of the most beautiful women I've ever seen. Were these beautiful women dressed in spandex? No not even close. What I did see was some Mennonite women dressed in traditional garb. The long dresses and high collars with little bonnets on their heads, kind of like the "Little House on the Prairie" look. These were some of the most Godly and virtuous women I've ever met. Does this mean I'm advocating that we all dress like grandma Moses? No, of course not. I'm just saying that modesty is a Godly attribute that I find lacking even in The Church. I'm amazed at what some women and men find appropriate church and non-church attire.

While they behold your chaste conversation coupled with fear. Whose adorning let it not be that outward adorning of plaiting the hair, and of wearing of gold, or of putting on of apparel; But let it be the hidden man of the heart, in that which is not corruptible, even the ornament of a meek and quiet spirit, which is in the sight of God of great price. For after this manner in the old time the holy women also, who trusted in God, adorned themselves, being in subjection unto their own husbands. (I Peter 3:2-5).

Men from years ago were no less sexually driven than they are today; but what they did have was the ability to keep it under check. A big contributing factor to their success was the lack of temptation, the lack of sexual stimuli. Back in the days when there was not this constant barrage of "porno queens on parade" to compare one's wife with, a man was more easily able to consider his own wife incomparable. Back in the days of proper dress code, when all you could see was a pretty face, you tended to focus more on the woman as an actual person, a person with an attractive personality, not merely an object of your sexual desire. Put this concept of loving and admiring one's own wife together with a God-fearing upbringing in a family home surrounded by loving parents and loving grandparents, and this is exactly what God had in mind when He set up the Divine Institution of the family. It was never intended for women to dress in a manner that has all kinds of flesh showing, constantly distracting a man's attention away from his wife. Now I know what you're thinking, "This guy can't be for real. He must have something against women." Well I don't have anything against women. It's just that not many people have the courage to speak the truth. The Bible is quite clear on these matters. And if you think the statements up to this point are "way out there", hold on to your seats! We are about to take a look at the other side of the coin. Let's see what Satan has done to the man. Satan— knowing that the man should be the spiritual leader in order for a society to succeed—knew he had to destroy the man. Besides attacking man's weakness in the flesh, Satan also had to attack man's ability to lead. And what better way to accomplish this than by, again, distorting man's focus. Satan whispers, "Forget family, forget God, forget responsibility, just focus on you". I've found that one of the stereo types of today about men runs true, "men never grow up". Today, the common male is a self-absorbed, egotistical child. With no role model available to teach leadership or Godly instruction, our men of today are a generation raised instead by Music TV, Monday night football, expensive toys, good times, and beer. They have no other drive than their sex drive. Their only vision for their future is one filled with money/success and women.

This know also, that in the last days perilous times shall come. For men shall be lovers of their own selves, covetous, boasters, proud, blasphemers, disobedient to parents, unthankful, unholy, without natural affection, trucebreakers, false accusers, incontinent, fierce, despisers of those that are good, traitors, heady, highminded, lovers of pleasure more than lovers of God; having a form of godliness, but denying the power thereof: from such turn away. (II Timothy 3:1-5)

Many men of today feel that "Marriage is something to be avoided at any cost". And "commitment" has become merely a word that one uses to please or pacify the current woman that one is with at the moment. When you take these men and put them in a marriage, it only gets worse. When they feel backed into a corner and all their friends are hitched, they bend under the pressure and walk down the aisle fighting all the way. Now you have a boy in a black tux promising to be faithful and loyal till death do us part. To this new-age man it's a totally unfamiliar world, he's so confused about his role or purpose. He has not a clue on where to turn, who's the boss, who's to be submissive. He does not have the answers to questions such as: "Am I to be sensitive or tough? Do I lead or follow? Do I cry or growl?" He becomes so petrified that all he desires to do is "run". With responsibility on top of responsibility, the pressure becomes overwhelming, and without a father or any man figure to turn to, he crumbles. The woman, by default and by her God-given desire to nurture a child, becomes the leader, sole decision maker, and controller. Then the man-senses click in and say, "Hey, when I was a boy I felt this way under my mom, I will become this again". So he returns to his child state, asking for permission to go out with friends, sneaking and lying to get what he desires. And what does he desire? What he always has: "to go play". This might sound too simplistic, but it's true. He wants his buddies around. He wants the freedom to play. He wants those toys that can only bring him joy and he will go to whatever lengths it takes to gain them. His only role then in the family unit is one of being a working child, a monetary provider. All other roles and responsibilities become, by default, the woman's and her's alone. The children see this, and what do you think they become: the girls become leaders and the boys become followers. With every generation this will only grow worse and worse. Some men, or should I say a large percentage, can't even exist in this scenario and end up bailing out, running back to their freedom and unpressured childhood, to the young girl friend and the "good old boys". So you see, God is not defaming women or "superiorizing" men. God has a format that works. Satan seeks to destroy that format. Satan uses the men and women of this age to accomplish his end. Yet, if you ask the "enlightened" world of today, they'll say they don't see this at all. They'll say, "In fact, things are getting better. Women are finally getting where they want to be. The sexual barriers are finally broken. The sexual taboos and guilt are finally gone. We can now express ourselves for who we are. Equality is just beyond the horizon. Through our own wisdom we are creating our utopia, experiencing our nirvana." Oh they just can't see it, Satan has blinded their eyes from the truth, and only turning to Jesus can open them. And we men, what are we doing about it? Let's continue and see what more the Bible has to say about our weakness.

When we scan through the many books of the Bible we find a peculiar scenario appearing time after time. Let's take a look at Solomon, Samson, and King David for starters. What did they all have in common? Well, for one, they were all men (which might be one of their major stumbling blocks). But that aside, we discover that—despite their great wisdom, knowledge of God, and character—they still fell prey to the age old sin of lust. These men communed with the Lord and were chosen by Him. One of them, Solomon, was even declared the "wisest man on earth" and yet, by the subtle sway and seductive words of a women all three were brought down in a swirl of disaster. The Bible, and even secular history, is laced with similar "war stories". Even as I pen these very words one of the highest ranking officials (probably in the world) could not resist the attraction of disaster, risking his career, reputation, and possibly his family for a few moments of fleeting pleasure. All common sense and rationale is put aside amidst the power of this incredible force.

Again, I know what you're concluding: "So it's all the women's fault. The poor guy just couldn't help it." No, No, then again, well maybe. Let's go back to Satan, that old serpent, the devil. We've concluded that Satan knows God's Word, and in addition to that, Satan has a plan. Satan's plan is to destroy all that God has established, to turn people to anything and anyone but the Lord Jesus, and of course, to try to take over the position of God Himself. Doesn't seem so hard to do, well to Satan it doesn't. So what does his plan entail? Well I've touched on it a bit already, but there is even much more to it than that. It's even more sinister and brilliant (if I can use that term in a negative way). Satan has observed and studied what he has to work with: humankind. He's had plenty of time to observe us and he has come up with some conclusions. Number one: men lust after women; men don't think straight when lusting; and when men don't think straight men make bad decisions, even stupid idiotic decisions. Number 2: God has established the man as spiritual leader in two areas: the spiritual head of his family—the family is the foundation of a nation—and as the spiritual leader of the local church. And number three: If I (Satan) can destroy the focus, vision, and will of the man, then I can in time destroy all that God has established. This all sounds good to Satan, but he still has one problem: the woman. He needs her to be his "tool" for she is the man's only weakness. It's like Superman and "cryptonite", so to speak.

"So what to do?" Satan ponders. "Well, men need stimuli in order to get this lust thing working properly, so I obviously need less clothes and more skin showing on the woman. I need a more forward, seductive, self-made women; a women who's in control and maybe who can even take control, yes, yes! Oh, but it's only 1920, 1930, 1940." Satan muses. "These people are too God-fearing, too reserved. The children have too much respect for their parents. And this society will never go for this type of woman. They're too devoted to their husbands and families and children, they have no drive nor ambition, they're just no good. I'll just have to be patient and slow and wait for the proper time, yes. But I can start now by working quietly on their children and their children's children", Satan plans. "Hum, 1950? No, not good enough yet. 1960? Yes, 1960, more like it. This drug idea is really working", Satan boasts. "Now let me persuade the women that raising a family and being a wife is second-rate and something to be ashamed of. Yes, convince them that there's something out there that they are missing. 1970, It's working! I've just gotta work harder on these kids now. Yes, X-rated movies, pornography, more drugs. Good! 1980, Oh my, Music TV, perfect move! I need more skin, more seduction, more sexual undertones. Now I just have to make it acceptable. Great, church attendance is dropping. God is now considered a "myth". Oh so wonderful! Evolution, what a great move if I do say so myself. Living together instead of marriage. Excellent! Now, if I can sell them on the idea that being a virgin and waiting for marriage to have sex is utter ridiculousness. Ah, did it! Great! The 21st Century, year 2000 and onwards, this is too good to be true: sex and rapes, divorce and child abuse. And women, oh my, they're almost perfect. Just a few more one-parent families and unwed mothers and yes, more self- satisfaction. And just listen to those TV and radio commercials! 'Come on down for your free consultation to have your breasts enlarged', I've got them saying, 'for that fuller natural look'. What could be more natural than what God has given them? Yep, I've fooled the 'little sillies' again. How about those penal enlargement commercials? I really have them hating what God has given them. This is so easy!"

Maybe Satan doesn't think "exactly" like that, but I bet I'm not too far off target. You see, Satan knew it would take time and that he would have to wait till the age was right. And it is working and will continue to work until we start to realize what we're up against. Remember, how he schemed, lied, and deceived back in the Garden: *"And the serpent said unto the woman, ye shall not surely die: for God doth know that in the day ye eat thereof, then your eyes shall be opened, and ye shall be as gods, knowing good and evil" (Genesis 3:4-5).*

Yes, it started way back then. Satan tried to tell us then, "Hey, don't listen to what God's telling you. You can be gods yourself. Just don't obey Him. It's OK". Even then he "used" the women and has taken away from her all of those wonderful qualities and also the place of honor that she once held. You don't think so? Well ponder this thought for a moment. As a Christian we know what the Lord's view of a perfect woman is, the "virtuous woman": *"Who can find a virtuous woman? for her price is far above rubies" (Proverbs 31:10).* Take a moment to go through the list of her qualities. Are they considered qualities to be sought after today? Does society portray a successful women as needing these qualities? Are daughters raised to be good wives or mothers? And is motherhood even a sought after or respected life choice? I think not. And from what I've seen, it's even looked down upon as not "fulfilling your potential", not "being what you could be". A women today with more than two children is greeted with pity for her "albatross". Ask yourself this question. Are we Christians even telling our daughters, "Honey, don't seek a career or profession, pray to be a stay-at-home mother and have a lot of God-fearing children and be the best wife you can be"?. I don't see it. What I do see is young girls being taught to shun and get as far away from house-wifing as possible. As a matter of fact, I can't think of too many girls in this generation wanting to—or even daring—to say, "Hey, I want to raise a family and be a stay-at-home wife". All we hear these days are things like "career, career, career"; "don't settle for anything less," "whatever you do, don't get married", "please don't get pregnant it'll ruin all your hopes and plans". Now I'm not saying that a woman can't have a career or job; but rather that, being a wife and mother should be viewed as just as good a choice—well actually the best choice—that a women can make. That's one thing that I have against the women's movement and their agenda. Equality in the work place is fine; freedom from sexual harassment, by all means—but when they look down their noses at women who choose something other than what they see as good, then all I see is hypocrisy. "We'll stand behind you as long as you pursue what we deem appropriate for a woman", they seem to be saying. Satan has certainly been very busy and has successfully turned every thing around. What was once good, he's made to appear bad, unwanted, belittling, and old fashion. Our young ladies are becoming sexual divas, self-centered and domineering. And in turn, as I stated earlier, our young men have become lazy, sex-obsessed, irresponsible, unwilling to grow up, toy and fun seeking, submissive to women and crumbling to every command. I know this is not a description of every man today, and I don't want to appear a kill joy, alarmist, way-out radical from some backwoods town uninformed and out of touch with society. On the contrary, I feel that if you read God's word and see His design for this world you will have to agree that we are "indeed" in a big mess. The woman is not to blame for the fall of mankind, the man is. Just as in the Garden: *"And unto Adam he said, because thou hast hearkened unto the voice of thy wife, and hast eaten of the tree, of which I commanded thee, saying, thou shalt not eat of it; cursed is the ground for thy sake; in sorrow shalt thou eat of it all the days of thy life" (Genesis 3:17).*

Eve was betrayed; but Adam sinned, and he "alone" was held accountable. We, as men, are all accountable for the state that we are now in. We've let it happen. We've sat back and watched as our roles and positions have slowly eroded away. Though I feel it's too late to change the world, I do feel that it's "not" too late to take back our homes and places of honor and take all of that burden off of our wives. You can agree with the Bible or toss it aside as so much nonsense—God has given us all a free will to do so—yet He has also made us "accountable" for our decisions. What will you decide?

The other day, I had no choice, when I accidentally overheard some women talking at work and they stated something that hit a cord. They said, (in very worldly terms which I will modify for your listening pleasure) "You show me one man who makes love, and doesn't just have 'sex'". Very interesting. Nothing about marriage and commitment; instead, selfish complaining about illicit fornication outside of the marriage bed. I found it quite profound, indeed, as well as profane! Never the less, is this true? Is this the typical male and female mind set of the twenty-first century? I'm ashamed to say it, but, I feel that in a lot of cases today, it is the growing trend. All you have to do is watch five minutes of any music television video, especially the "Rap" type music, and you'll find this image: rough, raw, and crude male figures with only one thing on their mind—quick, down and dirty sex...Now! No marriage mindedness, no desire to search out virtuous women. Instead, the sexier the girl is dressed, the more raunchy the men become. Why are men becoming so insensitive and violent towards women? Why is relationship, love and devotion, and marriage becoming so non-existent in the minds and hearts of them both? Remember: women need love and affection. The Bible tells us so. Yet, it seems that the women of today have been forced into a corner. Either get rough, tough, and ready—hide your emotions and needs, and become aggressive right back at um—or be crushed. Well, this leads into another master evil-working of Satan. One of the activities Satan likes best is perverting the Word of God and the will of God for His creation. As I pointed out a while back in this chapter, Satan knew he was bound by time and the morals of a particular period. But now that we've progressed so far—down, that is—he's able to let it flow full bore. Satan, knowing the needs of both men and women, and being one to hate passing up a good opportunity, came up with another set of plans. He reasoned, "Since women need love and affection, and since sex is not really that high on their list of prerequisites, I'll develop a place to turn to for all those who don't want to become the sex slaves of these cruel self-serving men. That is lesbianism, of course. Doesn't a woman know what another woman needs best?" Satan argues. "And the same goes for the guys—now that I have them to the point were all they really want is cold-blooded raw sex—why not put the guys together too?" The amazing thing is that Satan actually makes it sound logical. And to this world, that's exactly what it's becoming. Hey, he's even made it more acceptable and honorable to be gay than not to be. To add the finishing touches on it, he's created an atmosphere where if you don't accept it—pointing his finger at Christians—you're considered closed-minded, homophobic, and noninclusive. My friends, nothing could be further from the truth. We must always remember that God is bigger, better, and stronger than Satan. After all, He created Lucifer who became Satan. And, as God also did with us, He gave Satan a free will—to serve and follow, or to not. Satan, unfortunately, has chosen the same road as many of this world have. A choice that will ultimately destroy them. But that's another story. Always remember this: God never hates the sinner, just the sin. Whether it be murder, lying, lusting, or sexual perversion, He never closes the doors of redemption while you are living on this earth and He wants us all to treat everyone with that same attitude of love, not condemnation. As God hates stealing and lying, he also hates homosexuality—no more, no less—sin is sin, period. That's not my words, but God's. But more importantly, he loves the thief, the liar, the homosexual. What He wants is for us to first come in faith—just as we are, with all our sins and shortcomings—come in faith. Trust Him and He'll convict us of the rest. As I said before, God has given us all a free will to choose to obey or to choose to disobey Him—yet He has also made us "accountable" for our decisions. What will you decide?

CHAPTER 13

What does God say?
Hebrews 4:14

This could be a very easy chapter to write. Simply put, if God says, "Don't do it", then that's that! Don't "look", don't "touch", as a matter of fact, don't even "think" about it. Now I realize as well as you that, to the "babe in Christ", the Word of God can sometimes "appear" to be complex and grayish, leaving some people "choking on the meat". However, on the subject of lust, the Word of God is unmistakably clear, precise, and "sharper than any two-edged sword". You could spend eternity looking for loop holes only to end up with that very loop wrapped around your neck. So don't even bother looking for a grey, blue, or even green area. God's Word is all black and white when it comes to this one.

Wisdom, Oh to have the Lord's! Solomon had a great deal of it, yet, even he fell. What makes us think that we can even dabble without at least some wisdom. If there's one point God is constantly driving home to us, it is that by playing with fire, you "will", most definitely, get burned! In this case, the fire is a seductive women. In proverbs 6:23-33 we read:

For the commandment is a lamp; and the law is light; and reproofs of instruction are the way of life: (verse 23)

To keep thee from the evil woman, from the flattery of the tongue of a strange woman. (verse 24)

Lust not after her beauty in thine heart; neither let her take thee with her eyelids. (verse 25)

For by means of a whorish woman a man is brought to a piece of bread: and the adulteress will hunt for the precious life. (verse 26)

Can a man take fire in his bosom, and his clothes not be burned? (verse 27)

Can one go upon hot coals, and his feet not be burned? (verse 28)

So he that goeth in to his neighbour's wife; whosoever toucheth her shall not be innocent. (verse 29)

Men do not despise a thief, if he steal to satisfy his soul when he is hungry; (verse 30)

But if he be found, he shall restore sevenfold; he shall give all the substance of his house. (verse 31)

But whoso committeth adultery with a woman lacketh understanding: he that doeth it destroyeth his own soul. (verse 32)

A wound and dishonour shall he get; and his reproach shall not be wiped away. (verse 33)

Do we even have to go any further? We shouldn't have to, but sometimes a little pounding of The Word can go along way. So let's continue. In I Corinthians 6:15-20 we read:

Know ye not that your bodies are the members of Christ? Shall I then take the members of Christ, and make them the members of an harlot? God forbid. (verse 15)

What? know ye not that he which is joined to an harlot is one body? for two, saith He, shall be one flesh. (verse 16)

But he that is joined unto the Lord is one spirit. (verse 17)

Flee fornication. Every sin that a man doeth is without the body; but he that committeth fornication sinneth against his own body. (verse 18)

What? know ye not that your body is the temple of the Holy Ghost which is in you, which ye have of God, and ye are not your own? (verse 19)

For ye are bought with a price: therefore glorify God in your body, and in your spirit, which are God's. (verse 20)

This is an extremely important point that The Word makes here. There are many sins we commit in our lives, but the lust of the flesh (fornication) which is taken from the Greek word *porneia* from which we get the word "pornography", this sin not only harms our soul and fellowship with the Lord, but it also harms our own bodies. The Bible doesn't say exactly how, but it can be safe to say that sickness and disease have to be "up there" on the list. In verse nineteen we see how our body is indwelt by the Holy Ghost after our conversion to Jesus Christ and therefore actually becomes the "temple" of God! This knowledge alone should be enough to keep us from wanting to perform any harmful act against it. In verse twenty we see that our bodies are bought with a price (they have worth, contrary to what the theory of evolution would have us think). We are told to "Glorify God in our body". "Well, how do we do that?" you might ask. Well, by one not piercing it, tattooing it, committing adultery or fornication with it. The most important part of verse twenty is in the latter part which states that our body, our entire person, is God's. It is not our own, which only makes sense, since He bought it with His own blood on the Cross!

Marriage is honourable in all, and the bed undefiled: but whoremongers and adulterers God will judge. (Hebrews 13:4)

And in I John 2:16-17 we again read about the lust of the flesh:

For all that is in the world, the lust of the flesh, and the lust of the eyes, and the pride of life, is not of the Father, but is of the world. (verse 16)

And the world passeth away, and the lust thereof: but he that doeth the will of God abideth for ever. (verse 17)

Why does God keep speaking of lust? Well, common sense tells us that if it were not a big problem for us, then God wouldn't keep warning us about it over and over again.

The mouth of strange women is a deep pit: he that is abhorred of the Lord shall fall therein. (Proverbs 22:14)

Thine eyes shall behold strange women, and thine heart shall utter perverse things. (Proverbs 23:33)

Give not thy strength unto women, nor thy ways to that which destroyeth kings. (Proverbs 31:3)

And in Proverbs 7 we read:

That they may keep thee from the strange woman, from the stranger which flattereth with her words. (verse 5)

For at the window of my house I looked through my casement, (verse 6)

And beheld among the simple ones, I discerned among the youths, a young man void of understanding, (verse 7)

Passing through the street near her corner; and he went the way to her house, (verse 8)

In the twilight, in the evening, in the black and dark night: (verse 9)

And, behold, there met him a woman with the attire of an harlot, and subtle of heart. (verse 10)

She is loud and stubborn; her feet abide not in her house: (verse 11)

Now is she without, now in the streets, and lieth in wait at every corner. (verse 12)

So she caught him, and kissed him, and with an impudent face said unto him, (verse 14)

I have peace offerings with me; this day have I payed my vows. (verse 14)

Therefore came I forth to meet thee, diligently to seek thy face, and I have found thee. (verse 15)

I have decked my bed with coverings of tapestry, with carved works, with fine linen of Egypt. (verse 16)

I have perfumed my bed with myrrh, aloes, and cinnamon. (verse 17)

Come, let us take our fill of love until the morning: let us solace ourselves with loves. (verse 18)

For the goodman is not at home, he is gone a long journey: (verse 19)

He hath taken a bag of money with him, and will come home at the day appointed. (verse 20)

With her much fair speech she caused him to yield, with the flattering of her lips she forced him. (verse 21)

He goeth after her straightway, as an ox goeth to the slaughter, or as a fool to the correction of the stocks; (verse 22)

In verses twenty-one and twenty-two, the plot is evident. It's not so much that the harlot misled or coerced him, but that he lacked the "wisdom" to see the deceit and wickedness of her ways. The word "straightway" in the Hebrew is *pithom* and means "suddenly" or better yet, "instantly". It shows us that there was no time for thoughts about the consequences that may befall him.

Till a dart strike through his liver; as a bird hasteth to the snare, and knoweth not that it is for his life. (verse 23)

Hearken unto me now therefore, O ye children, and attend to the words of my mouth. (verse 24)
Let not thine heart decline to her ways, go not astray in her paths. (verse 25)

For she hath cast down many wounded: yea, many strong men have been slain by her. (verse 26)

Her house is the way to hell, going down to the chambers of death. (verse 27)

Heard enough? There's really nothing more to say. God really is quite clear: Don't do it, don't think it, and, by all means, don't look for it. You see, it's not that we don't know "what" or "how" God feels about our lust and sin, it's just that we can't seem to make ourselves take God's warnings seriously. There, my friend, is where a major part of the problem lies. We "know" about adultery, we've read about fornication. All these concepts are burned into our souls. But what we "do" with this knowledge is where we separate the men from the boys. Are you man enough, and mature enough, to take God seriously?

And while we're discussing adultery and fornication, there is one point that I would like to clear up: the difference between fornication and adultery.

*Now the body is not for fornication, but for the Lord; and the Lord for the body. **(I Corinthians 6:13)***

*But whoremongers and adulterers God will judge. **(Hebrews 13:4b)***

Now according to Webster's New World Dictionary the words "adultery" and "fornication" connotate basically the same definition:

fornication *n.* - *Syn.* adultery, illicit intercourse, unlicensed intercourse, promiscuousness, extramarital sex, premarital sex, incontinence, carnality, lechery, unchastity, lewdness, lubricity, libidinousness, licentiousness, venery, unfaithfulness, whoredom, harlotry, prostitution, concubinage, concupiscence, coitus, debauchery, libertinism; see also copulation.

adultery *n.* - *Syn.* unlicensed intercourse, infidelity, cuckoldry, extramarital affair; see fornication.

However, when we look into The Word of God, we find a difference. Here we find that "adultery" is something that can only happen if you are "married" and you have a sexual relation with someone other than your spouse. And we know, according to the words of Jesus Himself that "just looking" is the same as "touching"! "Wow!" you might say. But we know that since Jesus Himself stated it, it is absolutely true!

> *Ye have heard that it was said by them of old time, Thou shalt not commit adultery: But I say unto you, That whosoever looketh on a woman to lust after her hath committed adultery with her already in his heart. (**Matthew 5:27-28**)*

Now "fornication" is an interesting word in that it can be found both in the Old and the New Testaments meaning that it has both a Hebrew root and a Greek root. In the Hebrew, the word is *Zanah* which can be summed up as "going a-whoring, or whorish". In the Greek, the word is *porniea / porneuo* meaning "to indulge in un-lawful lust", and is also were we get our modern day translation of the word "pornography" or obscene literature. Please note that the key word in the definition of fornication is "un-lawful". "Well", you might ask, "just when is lust lawful?" Never! Lust is a sin no matter how you look at it. But since the word "lust" is a word that holds such an "intensity of feelings", a word that we men understand as "super super passionately desiring" when it comes to a woman, I am going to use "poetic license", to get the point across, by using the term "lust" when I say it is OK to "lust" after your own spouse. Yes, it's OK! It's OK to "lust" (super super passionately desire) after your own spouse. That's why God gave us these desires in the first place—to have a wonderfully joyous and exciting relationship with our spouse. So we know that lust is "unlawful" when lusting after someone or something other than what is legally or lawfully ours. But it is absolutely OK to have this same "intensity of feelings" when it is directed toward our spouse.

Which sin is worse: adultery or fornication? The point is really mute. They both are sin, and that's all we need to know. So, you single men out there, don't commit fornication, meaning "don't lust, and don't touch". And for you married guys, don't commit adultery, whether in your mind or with your flesh. It's simple. It's clear. And most of all, it's God's command! "So let it be written, so let it be done" (Yule Brenner, The Ten Commandments).

CHAPTER 14

The dumb things men do, (the end of reason)

Proverbs 19:3

Oh where do I begin? There's so many dumb things we do as men that I might have to write another book! I do have to admit though, this chapter was fun to write and eye opening at the same time. There's just so much ammunition out there, take for example spitting . Did you ever notice people who spit? Who are they? Well most start off as boys and continue this salivary ritual into manhood. A majority kick the habit when office etiquette dictates so, but some continue, determined to keep the tradition going. Think about it, when was the last time you saw a girl or woman hacking up a wet one? Putting physical conditions aside, what's the story? I spend a lot of time watching people. Not that I'm so perfect, but it's just fun to do. What I've found by observing people and spending a good part of my life being a man, is that we do dumb things. Why? Well from what I've gathered, it all has to do with wanting to be something we're not. Whether it is an attempt to be "cool" or tough or to appear to be an adult, it all stems from not being content with what we are. For the most part, I feel it's all an attempt to be adult-like, to emulate what we think we have to be to be accepted, liked, and loved. Society is constantly forcing children to grow up before their time. When being a kid is not "cool", a complete part of emotional development is sacrificed. I remember when I was a young boy I loved to play with my trucks in my family's back yard. It was a sad day when I had to start hiding my desire to play in the dirt, "because it was time to move on", I was told. And when the first guy on the block had a girlfriend, it was time for us all to "move on". Even though most of us still hated girls and thought they were "gross", we were forced to close that chapter in our life and again "move on" or be ridiculed. I also remember that overwhelming fear that came over me when I was the last guy without a girlfriend. "You mean you haven't kissed a girl yet?" Hey, I still wanted to play in my sand box! You must conform or be cast out. You have to smoke cigarettes, kiss the girls, and yes, spit on the sidewalk. Every year the ages get younger and younger, childhood becomes shorter and shorter. In turn we create a society with more and more emotional, physical, and mental confusion—a society that's lost a most precious part of living: our childhood. Where does that leave us now?

Here are some more examples of this "decaying of manhood" caused by deleting childhood. The other day my wife and I were in our family van with the kids. We were just coming home from a day of family fun, or as our kids call it, a "family day". The traffic was heavy this particular day with many people deciding to take advantage of this unexpectedly sunny, mild day for October. After coasting to a stop at so many traffic signals, we came across a particularly busy one and were privileged to roll to a stop right next to a car full of young men. They were your average urban fellows with their trendy hair cuts and booming music, loud enough to split an atom. As we sat next to them we couldn't help but overhear their rather loud remarks directed to a pretty young lady not much older than they, two cars over in a modest sports car. As they taunted and gestured their approval of her racy sportster, my wife questioned me, "Why do guys have to do that?" As I pondered the question my first thought was, "This would be a good subject to add to my book", and so I did. I find it so easy to look at fellows from this side of the bridge and say, "What immature bozo's". But after deeper introspection, I realized that would not be fair. Yes, I too at one time was one of those ridiculous fellows dangling my head out of a car full of guys, shouting out suggestive innuendos to unsuspecting blue-eyed ladies. So indeed it is a good question, "Why do men, boys, teenagers, whatever, seem to radiate to this type of sophomoric behavior?" I think before we get too deep into more "psycho babble", I'd like to poke some fun at the male psyche and what's really going through our heads. Let's start off with those young lads in the car next to me and my wife. What they're really hoping for is that a complete stranger, all alone, will for no good reason, comply with their taunts, gesture to them to pull over and then suggest having sex with all of them behind the nearest tree, say "Thanks", and be on her way. That could happen! Not! It's just amazing to watch us guys in action. Take the truckload of sweaty dirty construction workers going bananas over a girl walking by in a tight knit sweater. You'd think they never saw a girl before. Again as ridiculous as it might sound, deep in the depths of their perverted souls they hold to the thought, "Hey, you never know! She might just decide to stop in her tracks and say, 'Hey fellows, how about a roll in the dirt before lunch'". You see, with a man it doesn't take much to set our gears in motion. I've been at a counter with a sales clerk and all it takes is for her to say the simplest remark, remotely suggesting anything, like "have a nice day", and boom, it begins: "Hey, I think she likes me. Maybe she wants sex right now behind the men's footwear display". Pathetic I know! You want to hear some more; come on guys you know it's true. Take for example this scenario. You want to see men that are seemingly lifeless come to life? Just have a fairly attractive woman walk into a room and watch what happens. Men are born hams. They'll all be doing whatever their doing as "cool" and smooth as possible. And for some real fun just watch a pretty lady ask for assistance, or even better, ask to be instructed on how to do something. Grown men lose about twenty years or so in about five minutes! They'll go from middle-age men to gangly teenage boys in the bat of a false eyelash! The funny thing about us guys, and one thing women never figure out is this: Pretty isn't always a factor. As long as no one is around and the girl has two legs, two arms, and two you-know-what, all she has to do is just smile and we'll go into flirt mode faster than you can say, "My place or yours?" How about the looks men give! I've seen men almost twist their heads off of their bodies trying to get a glimpse of a well-endowed woman passing by; and the amazing thing is that we'll do it while holding hands with someone else. It's just amazing to see the same situation yield two completely different responses. Take again the two people at the check-out counter and add the ingredient of mutual interest. The girl gives a friendly smile and the guy responds in like manner. My friend, there are two completely different fantasies occurring here. Take the girl, she's thinking to herself, "Wow, cute guy! Walks on the beach. Romantic words of love. Curling up by a fire and deep talks of relationships and maybe marriage. Yes, prince charming coming to take me away." Now let's look at the degenerate side of the coin: He's thinking, "I'd love to see her in a string bikini! Look at those legs! I bet she's great in the sack!", and the Oh so typical, but predictable, "Wait till my buddies see me with her". Something seem wrong here? See signs of a problem developing here? Wonder why half, if not more, marriages end in divorce? Why men can't remain faithful? Why women are left holding the bag, so to speak, and raising America while the men (I use the term loosely) are running away back to their buddies and their bar mates. From seemingly harmless teenage boy play, to sex-crazed men, it's all part of the demoralizing and over-sexualizing of America, and the world. So why, as my wife so honestly put it, why do boys, and then men, lose all reason and rationale and think that this behavior can actually grant them some mystical, exotic sexual encounter when the odds of their fantasies ever becoming reality range from totally non-existent to maybe a one-in-a-million shot. Well, how does brainwashing sound? I know that's a little bit extreme, but if we dig deep we see that it's not too far off.

Let's start off with the simple stuff; number one being, "My dad does it". Well, maybe he doesn't hang his head out of a moving car to solicit and date, but he does admire a pretty figure. When the swimsuit issue comes out in his favorite sports magazine, he's not rushing to read the articles. When you were growing up as a boy, you remember his eyes trailing the bikinis on the beach. How about now? Does he rent "G" rated movies—or are the "R" rated and even the "X's" finding their way into your home? This all might seem harmless, but it's just another nail in the coffin called "lust". *"And ye fathers, provoke not your children to wrath: but bring them up in the nurture and admonition of the Lord" (Ephesians 6:4).*

And now let's also take a look at the friends these boys are paling around with. What's the peer pressure pushing to? Is it not, "Did you score last night? Did you go all the way? You're not still a virgin are you?" All of these forces, not to mention TV, the movies, and popular culture in general, are creating young boys, and then men, who have no picture of even a Godly mother to grasp and no father figure to teach them to honor and respect the opposite gender. *"And ye* shall teach them your children, speaking of them when thou sittest in thine house, and when thou walkest by the way, when thou liest down, and when thou risest up" *(Deuteronomy 11:19)*.

Is it any wonder why we have teens raping teens, date rape, and sexual violence of all kinds! In a world where God is only allowed in the form of a curse word, and where music videos are teaching them the new women's place, it's only going to get worse. The government has tried over and over again, program after program; but millions of dollars and a lot of good intentions will never work. You could have daytime, morning, and midnight basketball till you're blue in the face, but without Jesus in their hearts, homes, and minds, without two God-fearing loving parents, it "will not" and "cannot" work!

Train up a child in the way he should go: and when he is old, he will not depart from it. (Proverbs 22:6).

See then that ye walk circumspectly, not as fools, but as wise. (Ephesians 5:15)

The wise in heart will receive commandments: but a prating fool shall fall. (Proverbs 10:8)

Another profound silly story about men. The other day my wife and I were at a local automotive repair chain getting some new tires for our SUV. It was a beautiful warm fall day so all the shop doors were open wide. While we were waiting in the waiting room we noticed two young attractive girls, I'd say in their late teens to early twenties, one was a bleach blonde, and both were dressed, well, shall I say, modestly seductive. They were very talkative as we all took our turns pacing back and forth into the shop area to check on our respective vehicles. They related their dissatisfaction at having to wait so long, and we responded likewise. So you might ask, "What's the story?" Well, to add to my list of "dumb things men do" and how silly we act, this shop with its crew of approximately fifteen mechanics was, shall I say, so distracted by the young ladies pacing around that the shop almost came to a halt. "How do I know this" you might ask . Well, it was plain to see, but what ran the point home to me was when the young man who drove our vehicle out to us handed me my bill and said. "I'm real sorry, sir, that your car took so long, but the girls were driving us all crazy. I just couldn't concentrate." Needless to say, I questioned the lad regarding the integrity of the service that he performed on my vehicle during his lapse of concentration. He assured me that the wheels would stay on, and I'm happy to say that I'm still driving on all fours. You see my friend, this is just another example of the point that I'm trying to hit home with men (men, guys, boys, whatever you want to call us), we have a peculiar leaning towards the irrationally insane side. I often wonder how many women really know the testosterone-driven insanity of us men. God knows it well, and speaks of it often in His Word. Now, we men just need to know it, <u>and</u> confront it. Many might not see a problem at all, but from God's point of view there is a stumbling block that must be reckoned with if there ever is to be a life of spirituality, maturity, and, Christian growth. I could go on and on with these stories, and I'm sure you could dig up some yourself, but the point, though, is not the humor of these ditties, but their relevance to the problem that dwells, oh so prevalently, in men today.

CHAPTER 15

She Shall Be Called Woman!

Genesis 2:23

I'm sure you've heard the age old quote, "Women! You can't live with them, and you can't live without them". Sometimes it seems so true; but I prefer God's viewpoint. He created them to co-exist with man. If co-existence was impossible, that would mean He made a mistake. Well, we know that God can't make a mistake, so with that, I'd like to change that quote to "Women! You can live with them, or choose to live a life unto the Lord without them", to paraphrase what Paul suggests in I Corinthians 7:8. Because of God, it is possible.

I know, in this book it appears that women have taken some heavy hits. I've attempted to explain God's reasoning on it all, yet, I'm sure that many women will vehemently disagree with me. This is understandable, though I know that if you are truly a "Blood- bought child" of the Living God, the Holy Spirit will attest to these words in your heart at some point in your Christian life.

I have the highest regard for women, and more importantly than that, God does! What I'd like to do is devote this entire chapter exclusively to women: their importance in the economy of God, and their enduring God-given qualities, without which the world could not exist.

I know, I've condemned this present world over and over, but there are some good things that have been accomplished that are, indeed, noteworthy. For one thing, at least in the United States, women are finally beginning to be treated as equals with men: from voting, to sexual protection in the workplace, and it's long overdue. There are so many great minds that have, for too long, been overlooked and deliberately passed by just because they were attached to a woman's body. In our present society, there aren't many work places where you won't find women, from blue collar to white collar, working side-by-side with their male counterparts. Though I don't agree on what the Women's Movement has now become, I do champion the movement for its beneficial strides of progress in years gone by. We've all heard about those "sweat shops" and all the abuses women have endured in them throughout the ages. Without the devotion of the women involved in the Women's Movement back then, none of these victories would have been won. It's hard to believe that, not too long ago, women were considered no more than second-class citizens. Unfortunately, many of these types of travesties still continue unchecked throughout the world. There is still much work to be done.

Yes, women, at least in this country, have come a long way. What I'd like to look at now though is what does God say about women and how they are so wonderfully made. When you search the Scriptures, you'll find that the Lord is certainly not silent when it comes to women. Right from the beginning, God had a particular purpose in mind. In Genesis 2:22 we read, *"And the rib, which the Lord God had taken from man, made He a woman, and brought her unto the man."* We know that the man was made from the dust of the earth, but woman was made in a more unique way. God took, from something that He created perfect, "man", to form the woman. In Genesis 2:21-24 we read: *"And the Lord God caused a deep sleep to fall upon Adam and he slept: and He took one of his ribs, and closed up the flesh instead thereof. And the rib, which the Lord God had taken from man, made He a woman, and brought her unto the man. And Adam said, This is now bone of my bones, and flesh of my flesh: she shall be called woman, because she was taken out of man. Therefore shall a man leave his father and his mother, and shall cleave unto his wife: and they shall be one flesh.* In this verse, the word "flesh" in the Hebrew language in the Old Testament is *basar* which connotes being of one body, one skin, one self, nakedness. The battle of the sexes over equality should end right here. In marriage, God purposely designed the unique attributes of the man and the unique attributes of the woman to complement one another, to supplement one another, thus forming one complete body for the purpose of living together in harmony with one another and with God, and raising a family in harmony with God. Both the man and the woman's attributes are equally important to the marriage institution. When God said to the man *Cleave unto your wife*, He's giving instruction to draw from her the attributes that will make the union complete. Let's read on in Genesis 2:25, *"And they were both naked, the man and his wife, and were not ashamed"*, this truly confirms the perfectly balanced and humble union of man and wife. When it states that they were "naked" and not ashamed, we see all that is missing in marriage today. We see God's picture-perfect couple. The word "naked" in the Hebrew language is *arowm* which means bared, exposed, or half dressed, and speaks of Adam and Eve's acknowledgment of their incompleteness apart from one another. The statement and they were not ashamed tells us of their contentment in how the Lord had created them to be complete in one another— the woman equally as important as the man.

In the Scriptures we read over and over again how "Godly" women are to be admired and sought after. We see God calling on women to perform different ministries that only they can accomplish to His perfect will. Was not Eve in Genesis 3:20 called *"the mother of all living"*. If the Lord wanted to, He could have created man to give birth and carry on the race, but He chose not to, and He created woman to wear this crown. Look at Mary in Luke 1:28, *"And the angel came in unto her, and said, Hail, thou that art highly favoured, the Lord is with thee: blessed art thou among women"*. We find God using women in many ministries carrying out the work of the cross. In Philippians 4:3, *"And I entreat thee also, true yokefellow, help those women which laboured with me in the gospel, with Clement also, and with other my fellow labourers, whose names are in the book of life."*

All through God's Word we find "equality". There is never a time when God regards men above women. "Now wait a minute!", you women out there might be shouting. "How about all those words like, 'submit', and 'obey', and 'give reverence', and 'keep silent'?" Well, what about them? You see, this same misconception has gone on for eons, yet, the problem lies not in the Word, i.e. the Bible, but in the way certain words or phrases are inappropriately taken out of context, and our hypocritical bias (which we all dare to deny). Here's where the problem lies. Number one: designation. Number two: equality. And number three: contentment. Let's discus the first one: designation. There are simply different jobs designated for different people. Not for any other reason than that's how God wants it, and we have to trust that He knows what He's doing — and He does! — and then rest on that fact. If we dare to say He's wrong on this, then we might also then start to condemn the rest of the Bible as well; where do you draw the line? Where do you stop accusing God of being a liar. See what I'm getting at here? Where do you stop contradicting the Words of the Almighty Himself! Where do you stop inferring that you know as much as (or know better than) God? And remember, a body with two heads is a monster.

So now that we can acknowledge that the Lord God Almighty knows best,and that His Word is absolute truth, let's look at number two: equality. Where do you find, that because one person steers a ship and the other keeps it running, that one is above the other? Do not they both bring the ship into port together? They are both equal in importance as well as in necessity of operation — therefore all are equal in the eyes of God. In Galatians 3:28 we read *"There is neither Jew nor Greek, there is neither bond nor free, there is neither male nor female: for ye are all one in Christ Jesus".*

So now that we know that God assures us that we are all equal, let's explore number three: contentment. This is where the major problem lies: not being content with what the Lord has given. We all have jobs and we all have responsibilities. God made some male and some female, all have purpose, all have meaning. If you really concede that God knows best, then you have to be content with the job He's given you. In Hebrews 13:5 God's instructions are to *"Let your conversation be without covetousness; and be content with such things as ye have".*

Come with me now as we take an exciting walk through the Bible, taking a look at the women of the Bible, seeing how important they are to God's economy. First let's look at Ruth, a Moabitess who married a son of Elimelech and Naomi (Ruth 1:1-4). Was she important to God? I'd say so, since God even named a whole book of the Bible after her. Aside from its historical and genealogical significance, the book of Ruth deserves merit because of its ethical teachings. Ruth's refusal to be free, shows how she reverenced God and put

84

moral obligation at the top of her list. The Lord's hand guided Ruth into the field of Boaz (Ruth 2:1-3) and this wonderful story goes on from there. Ruth is also very significant in that she is the direct ancestor of the Promised One — The Messiah!

Esther is another woman with an exciting book of the Bible named in her honor. Esther was a Jewish orphan maiden who, because of her trust and obedience to Him, God elevated to the position of Queen of Persia; and in turn, God used her mightily to save her people (the Jews) from destruction (Esther 2:18-3:15,4-10). God is not intimidated by powerful women, He uses whomever, wherever, however He deems best.

We also have Martha, the sister of Lazarus and Mary of Bethany (Luke 10:38-41) who was very close friends with the Lord Jesus Himself; in fact, close enough to complain to Jesus about her sister's conduct (Luke 10:38-42) and also about His delay in coming when her brother Lazarus was sick (John 11:1-3,21).

How about the Marys? Where do I begin? First, of course, we have Mary, the virgin, chosen by the Lord Himself to bear His Humanity — chosen because of her humbleness and faith in the Lord. God uses the humble and raiseth them up! There is also Mary Magdalene who Jesus cared enough about to cast out seven demons (Mark 16:9 and Luke 8:2). She also was the first to learn of Jesus' resurrection (Matt 28:1-8). Then again, we have Mary of Bethany who was commended by Jesus for her thirst for the things of God (Luke 10:42), and who also anointed the feet of Jesus. We read of her great love and devotion to the Messiah in Luke 7:38, John 11:2, John 12:3, Matt. 26:7.

Oh, and let's not forget the dear and precious saint, Lydia. She was Paul's first convert in Europe, she was known as one who worshiped God , a proselyte. Her home in Philippi is believed to be the first Church in that city (Acts 16:14-15).

Look at Hannah, whose name means "grace and favor". She was one of the two wives of Elkanah, a Levite. She was clearly a Godly woman, she prayed for a son and vowed to give him to the Lord. God honored her prayer and gave her a son, Samuel, who was the great prophet of Israel. Incidently, when my wife and I were having trouble having our first child, it was the story of Hannah and her faith that stayed us both, so much so that we even named our child Jacob *Samuel* after Hannah's son.

How about Sarah? God promised her a son who we now know was Isaac (Genesis 17:15-27). In Isaiah 51:2, Sarah is referred to as the mother of the chosen race, the Jews.

Take Tabitha, a Christian woman important enough that God instructed Peter to raise her from the dead (Acts 9:36-43). Lets also not forget, Miriam, who was the first women to be a prophetess (Exodus 15:20). We have Deborah, a prophetess and judge over Israel (Judges 4:4), and Huldah, a prophetess who served Josiah and interpreted the book found in the temple as the law of Moses (2 Kings 22:14-20).

I could go on and on. The Lord has made it clear that all are integral to His Purpose, and all are equal. It all goes without saying that if the Lord Jehovah looks so highly upon these women, and all women for that matter, shouldn't we then, as Christian men, honor and uphold and praise all Godly women, *"for their price is truly far above rubies" (Prov 31:10).*

Looking through the Scriptures surely is telling! If you thought less of women, I hope this has opened your eyes a bit more. Women are what a man could never be. *"She considereth a field, and buyeth it: with the fruit of her hands she planteth a vineyard" (Proverbs 31:16).* She is mother, she is daughter, she is wife, she is friend. She can lead, and she can follow. She can nurture like no other and serve the Lord with all her heart. She's not greater than man, but she's also not less. Her virtue is full bloom when her heart is one with her Creator. *"She openeth her mouth with wisdom; and in her tongue is the law of kindness" (Proverbs 31:26). "She girdeth her loins with strength, and strengtheneth her arms" (Proverbs 31:17).*

"She perceiveth that her merchandise is good: her candle goeth not out by night" (Proverbs 31:18).

She can serve in capacities that a man could never attain to. *"She stretcheth out her hand to the poor; yea, she reacheth forth her hands to the needy" (Proverbs 31:20).* Her giving knows no limits and her labour is behind closed doors. She gives with all her fiber, and glows in the joy of her children. She can quench a teary eye and calm a frightened heart. *"Strength and honour are her clothing; and she shall rejoice in time to come" (Proverbs 31:25).* She can add color where there is grey; she can deliver sunshine when there's only the shade. Without her, this world would be a dismal dwelling place, I'm sure. I know it's been said in jest, but I dare to declare it as truth, Without a woman there would be no man .

Favour is deceitful, and beauty is vain: but a woman that feareth the Lord, she shall be praised. Give her of the fruit of her hands; and let her own works praise her in the gates. (Proverbs 31:30-31)

CHAPTER 16

Pornography: If we were Superman it would be our kryptonite!

Galatians 5:16-17 and II Peter 2:8

When I began writing this book I was determined to leave pornography out of it. I figured there was already too many books on it, and one more opinion was "one more" too many. However, I now feel convinced that I have to give it a chapter after all.

I believe that the average Christian male knows that pornography is bad; he knows it's wrong, and is evil. Understandingly then, the average "Girl Watcher" is probably not "addicted" to it. Lusting after the flesh and watching pornography doesn't "automatically" go hand-in-hand; we can thank God for that! So why am I adding this chapter in anyway? It's really quite simple: I feel that if girl-watching is your stumbling block, the pit can't be too far away. If you're an avid "Girl watcher", and even reading this book doesn't convince you of its evil, then what's going to keep you from taking the next step? If you like looking at women fully dressed, then it's only a matter of time before you desire to see them undressed. My friend, that step, in many cases, is the point of no return. Gaining victory over the lust of the flesh is one thing, gaining victory over pornography is a whole different ball game, and possibly the last game you'll ever play. I know that sounds corny, but it is sadly the truth.

So why, exactly, is pornography so devastating? For starters, let's take a look at the word itself:

por[nog[ra[phy 1 *(something) sold,* akin to perncmi, **2** *to sell (esp. as a slave, or for a bribe) 3* writings, pictures, etc. *intended primarily to arouse sexual desire.*

Looking at the dictionary it's plain to see why pornography is so devastating. I like the first part: *something sold.* This is interesting since something "sold" always has a price. Then looking at the definitions *slave* and *bribe*, this again is interesting because that's exactly what it does: it enslaves you. You no longer control yourself, it controls you. The term bribe connotes temptation. How is this all accomplished? It's all done through the third definition, through *writings and pictures, intended to arouse sexual desire.* If you read this book in its entirety, then you'll know who pornography is targeted at. If you haven't, shame, shame. I'll give you a hint. It's not women. It's really interesting when you think about it. Pornography doesn't affect women, nor is it directed at them. Sounds like Satan's been doing his homework, doesn't it? *"Let no man say when he is tempted, I am tempted of God: for God cannot be tempted with evil, neither tempteth He any man: but every man is tempted, when he is drawn away of his own lust, and enticed. Then when lust hath conceived, it bringeth forth sin: and sin, when it is finished, bringeth forth death" (James 1:13-15).* Oh yes, Satan knows exactly what he's doing and he does it rather well.

I remember when I was a boy I would often spend many a cold February morning duck hunting with my dad. (I bet you're wondering where this is going? Bear with me.) My dad and I would get to the hunting area well before daybreak, quietly setting out our decoys and putting on our face camouflage. We'd wait patiently in the bitter cold quacking away on our duck calls. It didn't matter how long we had to wait or how cold and rainy it became, because we knew that our efforts would be worth the spoils. You see, pornography is kind of like a duck vs. the duck hunter and his decoys. You see something that looks so harmless; you look down and see all of your buddies, the "good old boys", doing it; you think to yourself "what can it hurt?" So you join in on it too. And then when it's too late, you try to pull up and out! But you can't! Bang! You're Long Island duckling! All those "good old boys" were not real. They looked real, but all the camouflage and deception caught you before you could see it clearly for what it really was. Yes, not all the ducks get shot. Some are smart enough to pull away when they see their buddies going down, but the truth is, duck hunters rarely leave survivors. Remember, hunters are just human; Satan, on the other hand, uses "state of the art" equipment. He uses the best camouflage and the most seductive looking decoys you've ever seen. His calls are deceptively irresistible and; oh yeah, he rarely misses.

Think about this: If you've ever had to teach a Sunday school class or preach a sermon you know how important object lessons are. Sometimes they can make or break your lesson. And if you really have a good one, it is a great catalyst to get a message or idea across. Also, most people like object lessons, because it brings into clearer focus the point that you are trying to bring to light: i.e. the now famous hard-boiled egg/Trinity analogy. You know, The Father, Son, and Holy Spirit/shell, white, and yoke. All together, They are One; but separate Individuals.

Well, I think the Lord showed me a good object lesson (even better than duck hunting). The other day while driving the highways and byways of America, I was thinking about the "Titanic". I'm one of those people who is just entranced by the whole tragedy and its effects on us even today. The unsinkable ship, the maiden voyage, the captain's last stay at the helm before his overdue retirement, the lack of the proper amount of life boats, and the, Oh so many, other ironies. It all just screams out to the heart and soul: OBJECT LESSON !!

First off, having a vehicle to carry a thought is good, having a thought to be carried is far better. So what might be a "Titanic" thought? Well, "pornography" of course. So let's think for a moment about what is so "Titanic" in character about pornography? Well, for starters, let's just zero in on the "lust" of it and not so much the "iceberg" itself. You know we hear about addiction so much these days, and I've even discussed it many times in this book, but what makes an addiction so "de-mobilizing" is its crescendo effect, its sinking-sand, and its sinking-ship syndrome. Let's take the mammoth "Titanic" and look at it as a man sailing through this life. He feels strong, he feels confident; he's even been told that he cannot fail (sink). He knows the dangers, he's heard the warnings; but the fleshly builder of the vessel has convinced him he can tackle any storm and come out unscathed, even convinced him that he shouldn't be afraid to go ahead and tackle a few dangers every now and then. So what does he do? He sets sail with worldly confidence: "Life boats, who needs all those wimpy things? It's not manly! Go slowly across possible bad waters. That again is a sign of weakness. I'm going full bore!" So he sets sail, fully confident. His sensors pick up icebergs ahead: Porn, lust, temptation. "Hey, I've got not one, but many, water-tight chambers. I can't sink!" Then a little tickle presses, ever so gently, by pornography (whether through the Internet, by literature, or whatever, even by accident); "No problem" he declares. Then the water starts flowing in, ever so slowly. But still, "No worries. It's only over one water-tight section. One I can handle, even more". Then it's over section two, then three, then four. "Heck, I can handle much more than this', not even realizing he's slowly sinking. First, it's just a slight list, then more radical, ever so gentle but always downward. And then before he knows it, it's screaming in over the last water-tight chamber. Quickly he starts the pumps, frantically trying with all his might to discharge, what was at first, carelessly let in. The water is flowing in faster, and now it's mammoth weight is pulling down hard. "Send out the SOS for help!" But it's falling faster! And now with a heading radically southward, and then, once completely vertical, the bottom drops out! Deeper and deeper he falls with all that's recognizable of himself slowing disappearing. Deeper and faster! Now his character and total identity is unrecognizable, until in last desperation, the "sea waters" of lust and pornography cover him over. Yet it doesn't stop there. After the suction has finally dispersed, he still sinks deeper, yet quietly, to the depths of the deepest sea. Then on the ocean floor, all that remains is the empty hull that once was a great man; all his worth and splendor gone, all his purpose and future plans slowly terminated. And what about his loved ones? Yes, all of his loved ones were also caught in his great descent; relentlessly pulled down, unknowingly, by the overpowering suction. They trusted in him to carry them to safety. Yet, all that were close to him fell victim to the pull. Why couldn't he stop the flood waters? Why couldn't he stop the decent? Oh dear, that descent of a sinking ship that no man can restrain; that descent that can only be restrained by the Hand of God. Its pull, too mighty. It's weight, too overwhelming. For hind-sights sake, let's look back. When could the mighty descent have been halted? After the first tear of the iceberg? No, back further. Before the sighting, before the voyage?

Back further. If the captain only knew the weakness of the hull, the condition of the seas he would-be sailing; if his thoughts were more on the ships weaknesses rather than only on her strengths; then maybe a foundering ship she would not be.

Now, I know this is a little bombastic just to make a point, but a point had to be made. My friend and brother in Christ, don't tempt the waters of pornography and lust. Like those fabulous potato chips that you "can't just have one". The desire doesn't become stimulated until the first taste. Did you ever see that show called "The Little Shop of Horrors"? If you remember, there was this little plant that grew and grew by simply feeding it drops of human blood. The plant grew so large that its caretaker was overpowered by its demands and strength. "More! More!", it would proclaim, "Feed me, Seymore, feed me!"

Don't give in! Don't let Satan be the victor. Don't let him leave you worthless and ineffective for Christ.

> *This I say then, Walk in the Spirit, and ye shall not fulfill the lust of the flesh. For the flesh lusteth against the Spirit, and the Spirit against the flesh: and these are contrary the one to the other: so that ye cannot do the things that ye would. (Galatians 5:16-17)*

Remember Lot? He walked with God, raised a family; yet by living daily in and around the filth and perverseness of sin, his righteous soul became vexed. Day after day the "good" was worn away by the "bad". *"For that righteous man dwelling among them, in seeing and hearing, vexed his righteous soul from day to day with their unlawful deeds" (II Peter 2:8).* The heart that once walked in the Spirit now walked daily in "the flesh". Lot knew his sin and was ashamed for it. When the angels came to visit, he did not want his sin-sick world to overshadow them; so he tried without success to hide them in his home. The people pounded on his door until they prevailed (momentarily). You can't hide your sin, especially from God! No matter what or how, your sin "will find you out". Lot was spared, but the world that he knew was destroyed. The effects of his fleshly life were apparent by his wife's desire for the past and his daughters' corrupt thinking towards himself. He paid the price, and then some! My friend, "there is a sin unto death" (I John 5:16b). If God wanted to, He could have taken Lot's life, and taken him home. Thanks be to God for his "unmeasurable Grace"!

Take the Internet, for example, it is the mother of all icebergs. If there ever was a bane to the existence of lustful man, it is the Internet, bar none. For one thing, look at its characteristics. Number one: it is private, uninterrupted and uninhibited. Number two: it's at home where no one can find you out, no one can come into your private world. You can be a football coach dad one hour and perverted pedifile the next. Number three: it's unlimited. It draws you in. If you start out with just a curiosity for naked women, it silently says "why not take a peek at 'S&M', then beasteality, rape, and every other horrific filth you can imagine?" Your mouse holds the key. Just click click away. Now I beg you, if you can't control it yourself, then get rid of the darn thing! If you must have it for work, then get a filter; there are many good ones out there. Don't forget to give your wife the pass code so you can't change it yourself. Remember the Titanic! Do it for yourself, do it for your family, do it for the Lord and your fellowship with Him! It's not impossible, it's not unattainable! You *"can do all things through Christ which strengtheneth"* you. *(Philippians 4:13).*

Dear Brother in Christ, I'm not going to spend pages upon pages drilling you with the ills of pornography. The evidence is all in, and it's a 100% no-win situation. You know what The Word says, and you've seen the damage pornography can do. This is no game! The stakes are high! And the pain and suffering to yourself and family are devastating and often irrevocable. Maybe you think because no one can see you, and it's a secret that you've learned to hide well, you can somehow beat the odds. Simply put Brother, you cant! God sees all, and will in time, if repentance is not pursued, judge you with a mighty hand. Is it worth it? I know it's a hard row and probably the greatest personal struggle to overcome. Please, if you can't do it alone, then seek mature Christian help as soon as you can. Tell your wife of your secret struggle. Fall prostrate unto the Lord with a true desire for help and a genuine repentant heart and you will be victorious! God bless you!

Blessed is the man that endureth temptation: for when he is tried, he shall receive the crown of life, which the Lord hath promised to them that love Him. (James 1:12)

CHAPTER 17

Control,   Alternate,   Delete

I John 1:9

I hate to admit it, but I am becoming a "computer nut." It seems strange that it wasn't that long ago that I was one of those "anti-computer" people. As a matter of fact, when my church was contemplating getting its first computer, I was one of the only two people who voted against it. Things change, don't they? And with my tail between my legs, I later repented. Well that being stated, I now love computers. Just ask my wife! She'll gladly state her opinion loud and clear: "I think he loves that darn thing more than me." It's an on-going battle, so we try to compromise. The simple fact is, computers are so extremely efficient and convenient when it comes to writing. I can just go on for hours and not realize it's 2:00 am in the morning. Oh Well. Yes computers are handy, but like anything else there is a down-side to it all. Computers can drive you insane. Have you ever just completed the best work of your life and had it lost in a "lockup"? Wow that hurts, it's almost enough to drive a Christian man to profanity (almost). Never-the-less, it is frustrating, and when it does lock up sometimes the only solution is to hit the CTRL (Control), ALT (Alternate), and DEL (Delete) keys. Sometimes it works, but then, well you know the rest. I guess it would be proper to explain what a "lockup" actually is for you "non-computer" people (God bless you, you'll probably live at least five years longer than me). Well, a "lockup" is when you are doing too many things at one time. Computers are temperamental and they just get to the point when the input you're giving them is too much and too fast. They just need time to sort things out and digest all the information you're giving them. Simply put, they just say: "That's it! I've had enough! I'm stopping all forward progress." You can try pushing every button, turning every knob, but nothing will move. Sometimes it gets locked-up so badly that you have to just pull the plug and start over. When you get to that point, all that you have accomplished is lost and can never be restored; that's why I say, "Thank God for CTRL, ALT, and DEL."

I guess you are wondering by this time, "What in the world does all this have to do with *"Spiritual living in a sexual world* ?" I compare it to the tangled web of lustful thought patterns. For example, it's like this: you are at church and you're trying to think spiritual thoughts, you get a nod from your youngest child notifying you that he just spilled his apple juice, and at the same time some new young lady walks into church with a very inappropriately short skirt, dressed more like she should be at a nightclub than at Sunday Morning Service. This is what I call "lustful lockup". Too many thought inputs, too fast, and no time to properly set your thoughts in order. This can happen in many ways and in many different situations. You could be at work concentrating on a project, the boss comes in and starts riding you about yesterday's order that never went out, and at the same time you are trying to remember what your wife told you to bring home after work. It's "lockup" full bore. Different people have different ways of handling situations like this. Maybe you're the type who just explodes and lets his temper fly. Maybe you just keep it in and let it boil inside all day and then take it out on your family. Many emotions come into play in these kinds of situation, there is guilt in the case of the lustful look, there is anger at the screaming boss, and there is irritation about the errand your wife wants you to run on the way home. These are just a few. There can be many more, but they all have the same result. It would be nice if we had CTRL, ALT, DEL buttons to push. We don't, but we do have a way to get the same result. The Bible says in Matthew 11:28 *"Come to me all ye that are weak and heavy laden and I will give you rest"*. It also says in Psalm 55:22 *"Cast all your cares upon me"*. In Psalm 73:26 it states that our heart and flesh may fail us but God is our strength. Psalm 138:7 is another good one. How does all this apply to you and me? Try this next time Satan hits you with a triple. CTRL — Control any action that is contrary to God. ALT — Alternate your thinking by a quick prayer or reference to Scripture. A good idea here is to have a powerful "help" Scripture picked out beforehand that you can easily recall. I like Psalm 31:24 *"Be of good courage, and He shall strengthen your heart, all ye that hope in the Lord."* Next DEL - Delete any sinful thought immediately by confessing your sin. I know what you're thinking, "How can I do all this when all hell is breaking loose?" Yes, sometimes you can't, but you can at least control it by a quick sharp Scripture. Even if you just pull in the words "Control," "Alternate," "Delete." We have to remember, the longer sin resides in our soul the more damage it can do. The key here (no pun intended) is to act quickly. Get that lustful thought out! Delete it! You've heard of computer virus's. They sneak in through disguise and then slowly eat away at your computer hard drive until it's rendered inoperable and useless. It's the same with sin, especially with the lust of the flesh. It immobilizes and paralyzes the soul. You know, on my computer I have a program that cleans up things. Every once in a while I have to clean up old files and folders. If I've been on the Internet a lot, then there's plenty of "cookies" to be cleaned. If you don't periodically clean house, then everything starts to slow down. "Lockups" become more common. We as Christians have to do the same. If we go too long without confessing sin in sincere repentance, then we too can become sluggish and more prone to emotional "lockup". Just as my computer goes right back to full speed after a cleanup, so will we when we are living in the Spirit and not in the flesh. *I John 1:9* *"If we confess our sins, He is faithful and just to forgive us our sins, and to cleanse us from all unrighteousness."*

CHAPTER 18

How to get from here to there

A study in the book of Romans
Chapter 7:5-25

Well as you can figure, we are getting close to the end of this book. I've spoken about the "do's" and the "don'ts". I've told you what to do and what not to do, where to go and where not to go. I've explained the cost of this "sin of the flesh" and the chain of events that follow in its path. We know what causes it and where it can lead, the danger signs and the road blocks, the deception and the truth, the hurt and the pain to ourselves and the damage to our loved ones. What else is there? In the next chapter (the last chapter) I'll explain in great detail the source of the power that's needed to get from under the thumb of lust. Yet with all of this instruction, I would be remiss if I didn't include one very crucial ingredient. What are the means to get from here to there? The tools of the trade, the mechanics of this spiritual battle? In this chapter I'm going to try to explain the nuts and bolts of overcoming this sin that lies within us. Why is it there (not the lust of the flesh per se, but sin itself)? Why is there a battle, a struggle? Why do we fall over and over again into this constant "round robin" of sin and righteousness? If we know Who gives us the strength, and we know that the sin that we are committing is against our Lord, and we know it's hurting our families and our very lives, then why do we continue to seek sin's rewards? My brother in Christ, I've spent many years of my Christian walk contemplating and pondering this very thought. "It's as if God has given me a task that's too hard to bear," you might say. "Why would He give me a desire only to forbid me the exercise of it?" Well, it would seem that we have either a cruel God who enjoys our misery, or there's more to it than that and we need to investigate. Praise God, our Lord is a God of infinite grace, love, and compassion for His children. In other words, He couldn't, wouldn't, and would never give us a command without also giving us the ability or means to obey it. So before you go raising your fist Heavenward, you'd better think again. You see, the God we serve is unlike any so-called god Satan can conjure up. What I love so much about our Lord and Savior is that He became a man. (*John 1:14*) Yes, He left His world to experience our world, not that He wouldn't be able to know it without becoming a man, but I think to comfort our finite little minds He did this act, to bring it all down to a level which we could understand. He was tempted like us, He felt pain like us, He hungered like us, and He wept like us. You see, He "knows" the struggles. He "knows" the hurt. Yet, the amazing aspect of it all is that He endured all this without sin. Jesus was like us in His humanity, yet He did not sin — and most importantly, He

94

could not sin. He could have called down 10,000 angels with a single breath, but because of His love for us, He endured the pain. Now at this point I could go into all the doctrines and theology concerning all that took place, and why it took place, while He walked this earth and ultimately died and rose again. I'm not. Let's just say that there's much much more concerning this, and I implore you to read on in the Scriptures and discover all these wonderful workings of God. For now, though, I want to concentrate on my point, and that point being: God is not ignorant of our struggles and He has given us instructions to live and overcome in spite of our spiritual short comings.

So where to begin this quest for righteous living apart from sin? Simply put, there could be no better place, I believe, than with Paul and the Book of Romans, in particular, Chapter 7, verse 5 and onward. Now for those of you who have read this portion of Holy Writ, I'm sure you've scratched your head at least once (as I have) trying to interpret this seemingly complex lesson in the battle over sin, and the spirit. I remember lying in bed many a time reading those verses over and over again. I remember saying to myself, "What in the world is Paul talking about?" I would start to get it, then get lost again before I reached the end. This would often leave me angry, because of all the people in the Bible, Paul here seemed to be saying what I was feeling. He seemed for a moment like a regular guy beating himself up because he wanted to do good but could not. Wow, isn't that what this whole book is about, is not that all that we are really looking for? Could it be that this portion of Scripture holds the key to a life of victory? Yes, yes it does! You just have to look very carefully and the key here is, not too deep. Yes, the deeper you look for some mystical truth or formula, the farther off the mark you'll get. At this point let me comfort you with this: Paul does understand our plight. He feels our pain, and the best news is that the answer lies in those verses. So where to start? Let's start by looking at the Scripture itself.

Romans 7:5-25

verse 5. *For when we were in the flesh, the motions of sins, which were by the law, did work in our members to bring forth fruit unto death.*

Let's look at verse 5. I likened the first part "when we were in the flesh" as when we were unsaved and without Christ. And what did we do then? We sinned. How did we know we sinned? The law told us so. It was our "school teacher" the Bible says. What happens when we sin? We separate ourselves from God, which is spiritual death (this is the fruit of sin). Let's move on to verse 6.

verse 6. *But now we are delivered from the law, that being dead wherein we were held; that we should serve in newness of spirit, and not in the oldness of the letter.*

In verse 6 we are "delivered from the law." How? By a new life in Christ. We now live anew, and not by, and not bound by all that the law demanded, which we could never fulfill.

verse 7. *What shall we say then? Is the law sin? God forbid. Nay, I had not known sin, but by the law: for I had not known lust, except the law had said, Thou shalt not covet.*

Now verse 7. Is the law sin? Simple, God cannot create sin so the answer is "No". So why the law? Again, simply to show us what is right and what is wrong.

verse 8. *But sin, taking occasion by the commandment, wrought in me all manner of concupiscence. For without the law sin was dead.*

This verse here can be a little tricky, but let's take it slow. What Paul is saying is that because of the law he knows what sin is, and because of knowing what he can't have or do, it wrought in him all kinds of desire and covetousness. Like for an example, take Adam and Eve in the Garden, they did not desire the fruit of the tree until it was restricted from them.

verse 9. *For I was alive without the law once: but when the commandment came, sin revived, and I died.*

In verse 9, Paul clearly states that until he learned a law he felt free from it, but when the law was revealed, he realized his sin and because of his sin he became spiritually dead (separated from God).

verse 10. *And the commandment, which was ordained to life, I found to be unto death.*

In verse 10 the law "that was made for good", became a burden to bear because his sin became obvious.

verse 11. *For sin, taking occasion by the commandment, deceived me, and by it slew me.*

Here we see what we all face. Because of knowing the law we realize how difficult it is to abide by it, so it becomes a means of bondage to which we cannot free ourselves.

verse 12. *Wherefore the law is holy, and the commandment holy, and just, and good.*

Again he points out that what God has made (the law) is good, just, and holy.

verse 13. *Was then that which is good made death unto me? God forbid. But sin, that it might appear sin, working death in me by that which is good; that sin by the commandment might become exceeding sinful.*

Here all he is saying is that something that is good (the law), in doing what it is ordained to do, is unfortunately, revealing all the sin in his life.

verse 14. *For we know that the law is spiritual: but I am carnal, sold under sin.*

Verse 14 tells us the law is good, but Paul is not, and is a servant of sin because of his old sin nature from Adam.

verse 15. *For that which I do I allow not: for what I would, that do I not; but what I hate, that do I.*

Here's something we can all relate to. This is it, this is the bondage that we all deal with daily, we want to do good, but we don't. What we should do, we don't; and what we should not do, that we do easily.

verse 16. *If then I do that which I would not, I consent unto the law that it is good.*

Paul here kind of says, "Oh well, I'm thankful that the law shows me I'm a sinner". He's saying that "I'm not happy about my sin, but the law is doing its job never-the-less".

verse 17. *Now then it is no more I that do it, but sin that dwelleth in me.*

Paul is starting to get to the meat of the problem now. What he's trying to say is, "I don't want to sin, as a matter of fact, I hate to sin. It's not me that's sinning, but rather the sin that is in everyone of us. Sin is in us, its part of us, passed down from father to father."

verse 18. *For I know that in me (that is, in my flesh,) dwelleth no good thing: for to will is present with me; but how to perform that which is good I find not.*

Here's the problem. Now keep in mind, Paul is an Apostle chosen and appointed by God, yet he has this same problem that you and I face. He's admitting that he's a sinner, there's no good in him. He wants to please God and do good but he just can't figure out how! Sound familiar?

verse 19. *For the good that I would I do not: but the evil which I would not, that I do.*

Here is just a repeat of what he stated earlier, pointing out again how trying this problem is.

verse 20. *Now if I do that I would not, it is no more I that do it, but sin that dwelleth in me.*

This is another repeat, but this time of verse 17, (this is really serious to Paul) he really feels our pain.

verse 21. *I find then a law, that, when I would do good, evil is present with me.*

Oh dear Paul, here the sinews are beginning to come together. Paul is saying that, "this is a fact of life, even when we are doing good, 'evil is present in me'".

verse 22. *For I delight in the law of God after the inward man:*

In verse 22 it's again a repeat that Paul loves God and wants to please God in his heart of hearts.

verse 23. *But I see another law in my members, warring against the law of my mind, and bringing me into captivity to the law of sin which is in my members.*

Oh the proverbial "but". Paul sees another problem. He sees the remembrance of the law in his mind reminding him, and the sin that dwells in him, of that sin. Kind of like activating the "sin switch".

verse 24. *O wretched man that I am! Who shall deliver me from the body of this death?*

How many times have we all felt this way? How can I be freed from this messed-up mind and body that are constantly at war with each other. The good vs the bad.

verse 25. *I thank God through Jesus Christ our Lord. So then with the mind I myself serve the law of God; but with the flesh the law of sin.*

Finally, the answer we've all been waiting for, the climax, the crescendo. Because of Jesus my Lord I'm thankful! Why? Because God understands me, He forgives me. That's the "Key". Jesus forgives us. You see, without the atoning death of Jesus on the cross for me and you, we would have no "out". We would be forever spiritually dead with no way of escape. My friend, you can't live a life without sin, Sin is part of us until the day we die. Paul says that with the mind, his mind, your mind, my mind, when we become children of God through faith in Christ Jesus, our hearts and minds desire to serve and obey the Lord. Remember we now have the Holy Spirit dwelling within us, and there can be no sin; but unfortunately the flesh, our old sin nature from birth, will always serve the law of sin. Simply put, when you're in the spirit (in fellowship with God by seeking forgiveness) you won't fulfill the lust of the flesh (sin). Yes it's true, you can't sin while in the spirit, so the key is to stay in the spirit. (*I John 1:9*)

I know you were hoping for some greater revelation, some greater formula for success. I know you're thinking, "Is that it? Where does that leave me? Do I just keep sinning and have fun and then ask for forgiveness each day?" No! Point number one. You won't have any "fun". You'll surely be miserable. That's bad—but, you see the good part is that God understands. That weight that crushes our joy in Christ has been lifted. The Christian experience can be attained! But it doesn't end there. Yes, God understands, that's true, but that doesn't mean that you can just wallow in your sin. No way! God wants to see your desire, your effort, your willingness to serve Him, your fight to live holy unto the Lord. He wants to see you trying — really trying. Yes sin is in us — but, *"greater is He that is in you than he that is in the world"*. Maybe some of us will progress faster or slower than others, but the point is: there must be growth! I tell you what, since we all like a formula to follow, try this one.

A) Start each day in prayer. "Lord, help me to keep my eyes forward and upward."

B) Repent and ask for forgiveness after each and every sinful encounter. "Lord forgive me, I should not have looked, help me to not look again. In Jesus' name".

C) Read you Bible — "Everyday"! If you don't know where to start, try this: on the first of the month read Proverbs Chapter 1; on the second read Proverbs Chapter 2, on the third Proverbs Chapter 3; and right on through the month. I like Proverbs in particular because it deals heavily with the sins and lust of the flesh.

D) Spend time alone with God — walk with Him, talk with Him. Tell Him how you feel, don't worry He can take it. He knows even your evilist thought.

E) Important, GO TO CHURCH! If you don't have one, then find one. No frills here, just a simple Bible believing Church grounded in the Word.

F) Last but not least, fellowship with mature Christian men who are not struggling with your particular vice.

You know it's like this: feed your soul and it will grow strong and repellent to the flesh and sin; starve your soul and you'll have no strength to keep down that sin nature. To counter the daily barrage of the world that we must endure we must counter it with massive doses of vitamins – "B" for Bible, "R" for repentance, "F" for fellowship, and "G" for God's grace that keeps us going from day to day. In chapter 19, the last chapter of this book, you'll find the cord that binds all of this up. I strongly recommend you read it. I know it seems as if this should be the end of this book, and to be honest with you maybe this chapter should have been last, but like I said early in this book, "This has been a 'work of the heart'". I've not penned a word without prayerful thought. I feel the Lord has led me through these writings and if nothing else it has helped me understand the Christian journey a little better.

CHAPTER 19

The answers lie at Via Dolorosa (The Way of the Cross)

I John 2:1-2

Throughout this book I've run the gambit of reasons for this thing called "lust", from the ills caused by a sin-sick society to the effects of adolescence growing up with pornography; and if I left you in this state of "cliff hanging" without a "bungee" cord, I would be no better than your typical politician. Pointing out all the problems without producing any solutions, that's man's way, but, praise be to God — our God, the "only" God — He always has solutions. He would not, and for that matter, "could not" hand you something and say, "Hey, deal with it".

A man's heart deviseth his way: but the Lord directeth his steps. ***(Proverbs 16:9)***

For his God doth instruct him to discretion, and doth teach him. ***(Isaiah 28:26)***

Trust in the Lord with all thine heart; and lean not unto thine own understanding. In all thy ways acknowledge Him, and He shall direct thy paths. ***(Proverbs 3:5-6)***

My friend, you can be whole! You can have victory! You can be the man, husband, father, and Christian that the Lord wants you to be. How do I know this? Well for one, I know the Bible tells me so, and for another, I know, because God has told me. I wasn't going to add this, but I'd like to share why I wrote this book. As strange as it might seem, I did not know the answers to this problem when I started writing this book. I knew what I was feeling was real, and when I started talking with other Christian men, I discovered that I was not alone. I felt the Lord calling me to share these feelings and struggles, and through a time of deep inner introspection and soulful groaning, I began to write. I'm not some great psychological scholar, nor some learned theologian, I'm just like you. I'm a man who's seen what I've shouldn't, wanted what I couldn't have, and learned things that were not true. We can find many people, places, and things to blame, but in the end, it is plain to see that it is we ourselves who hold the smoking gun. What's in the past is over and done. What we've seen or desired has already done it's damage. We can lament over our state, or confess it and move on!

*Though he fall, he shall not be utterly cast down: for the Lord upholdeth him with His hand. **(Psalm 37;24)***

*My flesh and my heart faileth; but God is the strength of my heart, and my portion for ever. **(Psalm 73:26)***

*They that sow in tears shall reap in joy. He that goeth forth and weepeth, bearing precious seed, shall doubtless come again with rejoicing, bringing his sheaves with him. **(Psalm 126:5-6)***

*He shall deliver thee in six troubles: yea, in seven there shall no evil touch thee. **(Job 5:19)***

*If we confess our sins, He is faithful and just to forgive us our sins, and to cleanse us from all unrighteousness. **(I John 1:9)***

*It is of the Lord's mercies that we are not consumed, because His compassions fail not. They are new every morning: great is Thy faithfulness. **(Lamentations 3:22-23)***

The Lord's mercies are new "every morning"; that's one of the messages that God has shown to me. Tomorrow is a new day! You "can" begin again! In fact, is that not one of the greatest attributes of being a Christian: being able to start over and over again! I started out writing down what I've been through and what I've observed. I relied only on what God would reveal to me. I remember saying to myself: "Lord, how can I write a book to help these men and their wives out there when I only know of the desire and grip of this 'thorn' myself?" Yet I kept writing, and would not write a single word without first starting in prayer. To me, this has been a journey, and only now has the light of my destination finally lighted ahead. This journey, that started way before I was a teen, was not for nought. My friend, God never sends you out without a purpose. As with Joseph and his journey from incomprehensible and seemingly unjustifiable misfortunes and calamities, to his exultation to heights and blessings unnumbered, you can see the moving of the hand of God and His omniscience (all knowing) power. I believe, for myself, this journey has not been in vain, though I'm not saying that God ordains sin, but rather that He uses all things "working together for good". *"And we know that all things work together for good to them that love God, to them who are the called according to His purpose" **(Romans 8:28).*** Whatever you learn through your walk in Christ, if you keep it locked inside of you because of pride and personal shame, then you are stealing away the wisdom given to you by God Himself from those who need it most.

Blessed be God, even the Father of our Lord Jesus Christ, the Father of mercies, and the God of all comfort; Who comforteth us in all our tribulation, that we may be able to comfort them which are in any trouble, by the comfort wherewith we ourselves are comforted of God. For as the sufferings of Christ abound in us, so our consolation also aboundeth by Christ. (II Corinthians 1:3-5)

To let another person suffer, when you hold the comfort in your hands, is unmitigated selfishness. Well enough of all this sentimental groaning, for I would, in fact, be committing that very act of selfishness if I did not complete this book with the wisdom that I've been given through experiences.

I wish I could just give you a simple prayer or pill to recite or take. I wish that I could simply say "Read chapter so and so of a particular book of the Bible", and all your problems would be solved. But as you probably already guessed, it's not that easy; yet, that's not saying it's impossible. As a matter of fact, I believe that with sincere faith and commitment, your freedom can be just around the corner.

If there's one thing I've learned about God, is that you never stop learning. Just as I was about to pen my finishing notes on this book, I was given a gruesome revelation, but a revelation none-the-less. Both my sons, like most typical boys, have a fascination with creepy crawly bugs with one exception: my eldest son, Jacob, has a nails-scraping-across-a-blackboard fear of bees, which is not unjustified since he was stung twice before he was seven years old. Whenever there's anything even remotely resembling a bee flying around, he goes ballistic. So me, wanting to be the good "home-schooling" dad, decided that if I could find a dead bee and bring it home and have my son examine it under his microscope, he would learn about bees and how they live and what purpose God has for them and this might lessen his fear. And so I began my search for a bee. I decided to wait until the Fall when the bees and bugs get that sort-of drunk demeanor to them. Well, one day, while getting gas, I found the perfect specimen on the gas station parking lot. He was still alive, and so to protect myself I figured, "Let me just kill the thing to save a lot of pain". I pulled out my pocket knife and, with the skill and dexterity of a surgeon, I decapitated the beast, figuring "Surely, that would put an end to his little life". Well, to my surprise, he didn't die; well, not until about five hours went by. I couldn't believe it. Every time I would check on him by poking him with my finger, he would come alive, thrashing his stinger at me with the voracity of a banshee. At one point he actually righted himself and was attempting to fly — he didn't. As I watched in bewilderment at this killer's nervous system's reaction to stimuli, I knew there was a message in here somewhere. There was. It jumped out at me almost verbatim: sin is not something that's learned; it is our "nature", that is, our "sin nature", our tendency to do bad over good. It's not something that you can eliminate by cutting out its source. Like the bee without the head, sin does not need to be fed or controlled by outside temptations. As I watched the bee, it kept fighting and stabbing away without even seeing what was coming to harm it. The natural in-born reflexes can't be stopped. You see, if for example you could take a child from birth and shield him from every evil and corrupt thing and only expose him to Godliness and Bible cartoons, would or could that child still have a desire to lust when he was grown? Would he not still be a sinner? Yes. *"For all have sinned, and come short of the glory of God" (Romans 3:23). "As it is written, There is none righteous, no, not one" (Romans 3:10).* You see, the one fact that we have to face is that we can never be without sin in this life. The desire to be bad will always be stronger than our desire to be good. For those of you who have children, did you ever have to "teach" them to do bad things? No, they do them naturally. Do they do good naturally? If your kids are like mine, you know the answers. Goodness has to be instilled, and over time, with the guidance of the Holy Spirit, and in the power of the Holy Spirit, the desire to do good will overpower the bad. I have a theory that I feel very strongly about. I call it the theory of potential sin, or if you like, the "sin potential". What that means is that everyone has the potential for all kinds of evil, from murder to stealing to sexual perversions of every kind. What keeps most of us from acting on these things is our upbringing, our relationship to God, and the society we live in. Now, not everyone is prone to every sin to the same degree. Some may have more of a leaning towards being a potential, say, violent person with a bad temper. This type of person, given the wrong upbringing and the right situation, might actually murder someone. Now I'm not saying that everyone with a bad temper is a potential murderer, but that it might be easier for them to have at least thought about it. Think about yourself on a hot August day, stuck in traffic, the *AC* not working, and the guy next to you keeps blowing his horn and then cuts you off. Haven't you ever in the heat of rage thought, even for a millisecond, "Man, if I had a gun"? Admit it, we all have, to one degree or another. And remember, the Bible says that even thinking it is the same as acting on it. What this all boils down to is that we are sinners and we always will be. If you were fortunate enough to be raised in a God-fearing Christian home, and kept away from all exposure to pornography and evil, then you probably won't have as much of a problem with lust as the person who has a genetic tendency to more than normal sexual desires. Put that person in an unsaved promiscuous home, throw in puberty and pornography, and you have the makings of a person extremely vulnerable and prone to the sin of the lust of the flesh. If you are reading this book than you probably fall into this category. The battle won't be easy, but it can be won!

Let's start off with the "biggie": do you want to stop this lust thing? Now this might sound like a silly question. You're probably saying, "Of course I do". Do you? Do you really want to stop? The point I'm driving at here is, do you like it?

Do you like looking? I'm sure if you asked the average American male, he'd say "oh yah!!" I'd say, for a lot of men, it's even like a hobby: "girl watching". This might be the most difficult obstacle to overcome. How do you stop doing something that you like doing? There is a fine line here, because I know, even though you like it, you know that you have to stop! So the "trick" is, if I can use that term, is making the desire to stop, greater than the joy you get in "looking". How is this done? One way, and one way only: you must ask the Lord to start dealing with you about this sin. "What's so big about that", you might say. Well, it's "very big" and for this reason, when you get down on your hands and knees and ask the Lord to really start dealing with you in this area, He will do just that! He will start tying on consequences and problems with every look and every flirtatious endeavor. Simply put, it won't be fun anymore. Every time you watch a movie, or look through a magazine, God will start letting you know that He's watching. Not that He wasn't watching before, but rather that, before, you weren't responding and had no desire to stop. So God would let nature take its course until you got yourself in so deep that you had to come begging for help, which most of the time was after the fact and the damage was done. Too easy? Just try it! I bet there's even a couple of you saying, "I don't know if I want to pray that prayer". Understandable, but let's weigh it out. You know what's happening or will happen to your family and job and relationship with your wife, or girl friend. You know that your testimony as a Christian and your work for the Lord is being hindered. What's it gonna be? What's more important? I'll say it again and again, it's not "just looking". So many men that I speak with hand me that line to justify their lust. OK, enough fist pounding, let's go on.

Devotion time — time with the Lord Jesus in His Word, because Jesus is the Living Word! And don't just read the "Daily Bread" or some short devotional, read the Bible and "meditate" on The Word — at least twice a day, one half hour each! And go ahead and actually memorize your favorite verses so that you can repeat them to yourself in time of need. All this will help ensure the communication lines are open between you and God. And make sure you pray before each devotion time, both to confess your sins, and to ask God's guidance in understanding what you are about to read — to open your heart to accept His teaching! Being in fellowship with Jesus, heart-felt fervent prayer, Bible reading and studying, fellowship with other believers is the key!

The TV! Wow, I could write a chapter just on this one. It's the worst. And don't tell me you just watch it for the sports channel. Did you know why us guys like flipping the remote constantly? What are we looking for? What do you think, Girls! Think about it. What will put a pause in your rapid fire channel changing? Nothing but a bikini clad vixen or maybe a good car wreck. Why do you think every product for men has a "Babe" in it (that's guy talk for a nice looking young lady for all you wives). Those beer companies are not stupid; do you think you would stop for a millisecond to watch one that didn't have a "Babe in it. The TV is bad! There is just no other way to put it. Personally, at the moment, mine is disconnected. That's right. No cable at all, fuzz! If I want to watch something, I can rent a "G" rated movie, maybe a "PG". This does many things. Number one, it gives you no excuse for not reading the Word. It frees up time for communications with your wife. Yes you do have to talk, it's part of the wedding contract (it's in the small print). You will also have time to spend with your kids. And best of all, it's one giant reduction in the temptation department! Now this might seem extreme for some of you, but I feel if you're really serious about this, you'll take the plunge.

Moving on, I can't emphasize enough the utter importance of prayer time — daily holding yourself and others up in prayer before the Throne of Grace. Set aside a scheduled time each day for heart-felt prayer — not just a superficial prayer before you fall asleep at night just to get it over with. But actually make a designated time to "talk" one-to-one with the Lord! Discuss your feelings, your problems, confess your sins, ask Him for His guidance and strength, thank Him for answered prayer, thank Him for His many blessings to you, thank Him for His shed blood on the Cross, thank Him for your salvation, and praise His Name!

And in those frustrating times — and yes, it will occasionally happen — when you don't feel like you are connecting, when your prayers seem insincere and hollow even to your own ears, don't be afraid to actually get down on your knees. Getting yourself to "willingly" get on your knees — that act of humility in itself often times is enough to change your attitude and allow you to be ready and willing to let go of whatever current sin or pride is keeping you from being serious. You see, confessing one's sins is actually a three-fold operation. You must not only confess your sin with your lips, but also repent of it in your mind (change your mind about it and finally admit to yourself that it was truly wrong, and that you don't want to keep doing it), and then also agree in your heart to yield to God's judgment on the matter (give it over to the Lord and rely on His help to overcome it). Getting past that pride barrier, changing your attitude, and truly confessing your sins will then set you free to pray seriously, to be back in harmony with and talk one-to-one with God again.

Now in addition to that daily set-aside time, say a brief silent prayer when your feet hit the floor in the morning, before you eat each meal, as you get in your car, as you are punching the time clock both in the morning as well as when you leave for home, as you are greeting and speaking to people during the course of your day, before you go into a meeting, etc. I'm sure you get the picture, before or as you move on to the next plateau of your day, pray! Be in constant fellowship with and stay in constant communication with the "source" of your strength — God!

And if you're not going to church, then find a good Bible-believing one and go! Get involved! Saturate yourself with the Lord Jesus and His Word! Make a new life for yourself — a new life centered around the Person of the Lord Jesus your Saviour! He's the One who loves you! He's the One who died for you! Make the Person of the Lord Jesus come alive to you! Get to know Him on a personal level. Go to Bible study. In fact, go to all the church services that are available. Reach out to other Believers, stay behind after the church services to talk to a few of them. Take them on as your friends, invite them to your home. Become a part of the men's fellowship if they have one. Speaking about fellowship, do it! Stop hanging around with the guys at the office or shop and find some sound Christian men. Personally, I find it extremely helpful to fellowship with brothers who are more spiritually mature than myself. You'll always tend to be like those who you are hanging around with, and moving up is always better than moving down. Become the spiritual leader of your family, not in name only, but in action! Bring your wife along with you to church (and of course your children too). There is such a special blessing when a man and his wife are sitting side-by-side being fed on the Word of God together! This is the spiritual epitome of what God had in mind for the marriage union! You, your wife, and the Lord Jesus in sweet fellowship together!

Now comes the hard part. How about the beach and the neighbor's pool and all those girls at the local mall. "How do I exist with out looking?", you ask. For starters, if you've laid the foundation, then it won't be as difficult as you may think. My motto is "be prepared". If you know you have no choice and you have to go into the lion's den, i.e. the beach, then be prepared. Pray and pray again before you get there, during, and after. Ask the Lord to give you the strength and desire to not look. Remember way back when I said it's a learned response? Well you have to "un-learn" it. In time, it will become easier and more natural to "not" look than to look. It's going to take time, and don't be upset if you fall here and there. One thing the Lord has shown me is that He understands our struggles and He honors even the littlest effort. As long as you're earnestly trying He's happy. And be prepared, once you set out on this mission Satan will be there with bells on. And if he has to he'll have even "naked" ladies walking up and down the beach. Remember that's BAD, right? I know I've thrown a little humor in here and there, but I don't want that to take away from the seriousness of this sin. If you continue in it, you will never ever be what the Lord has in store for you. You will never know the true *"peace of God that passeth understanding"*. Maybe you won't go too far and have an affair or one night stand, but a good percentage of you will. And at that point the damage has already been done and the pain has been inflicted. Don't look! And if you do make contact, which will occasionally happen, quickly turn away. If you've thought about her for more than a micro second, right then and there, ask God for forgiveness. Yes, and there's even more. Don't go at it alone. Share your struggle with a *trusted* mature Christian friend, preferably a male friend. It's always good to have a prayer base of at least two people, with one of them being your wife. It's also important that you tell your wife of your struggle and of your desire to beat it. This might not always be

106

possible, depending on the maturity of your spouse. Don't be too critical of yourself, but also don't be too lenient either. A good measuring stick to go by is to make sure you are always moving forward. Yes, you may fall back two steps, but that should always be countered by three steps forward. Another point is knowing your limitations, like when I mentioned about avoiding the beach, I wasn't kidding! It's like, if you know that you are allergic to poison ivy, do you purposely walk through a known poison ivy patch? Of course not. So why would it seem strange to avoid the beach to protect yourself from that hazard. If you think of it, the consequences of the lust of the flesh far outweigh the itchy rash of the ivy. Unfortunately, a major hindrance in this area always boils down to pride, which God hates most of all. *"The fear of the Lord is to hate evil: pride, and arrogancy, and the evil way, and the froward mouth, do I hate" (Proverbs 8:13). God also warns us that "Pride goeth before destruction, and an haughty spirit before a fall" (Proverbs 16:18).* So often we are more concerned about how we are perceived by the world than what the Lord will see in us. I know it's embarrassing to admit "I can't control my eyes so I don't go to the beach". It's humbling no doubt, but again weigh the cost. Face it, just by living in the sin of pride you are headed for trouble. Just as with any vice, is not the first step admitting that you have a problem? Avoiding the temptations and knowing what tempts you is half the battle. I've heard stories of youth pastors or leaders that entered into a ministry with the best of intentions, only to later fall into an improper relationship with a young teen because they did not know, or admit to, their own weakness and did not acknowledge the power of the flesh. This might sound unfathomable or horrific, but this kind of behavior does and has happened. If you have a problem with lust, then by all means, do NOT go camping with a bunch of teenage girls. This is not the ministry for you.

My friend, there are no easy paths when you are fighting the ways of this world. There are no places to hide from the sin and the guilt. Wherever you go, the temptations will always be there. But just as the evil is always there, so is the Father, the Son and the Holy Spirit, working, guiding, and comforting! We are so fortunate to be living in this wonderful age of Grace where God's judgement is slow and His love abundant. He knows what it's like to be human, He knows what makes us tick. He's patient and kind and only wants the best for his children. If we stumble, He'll pick us up; if we stray, He'll turn us around. The Lord has a will and a plan for each of us, no matter how rich or poor you are. He's given us a free will to make our own choice to follow His lead. We are not puppets on a string that have no say or voice in what we become. Just as a parent hates to see his child take the wrong road, the Lord grieves when we choose not to go His Way. Oh, to live in God's perfect will and to know the blessedness of His perfect peace. On this planet there is no greater joy obtained than to be in the path that He has chosen for you to travel. Like our brother Paul, "Let us run the race that is set before us and finish the course" looking only for those distant and comforting words of our Lord, "Well done, my good and faithful servant!"

His Lord said unto him, Well done, thou good and faithful servant: thou hast been faithful over a few things, I will make thee ruler over many things: enter thou into the joy of the Lord! **(Matthew 25:21)**

"Enter Thou into the Joy of the Lord", what wonderful words!

The victory is in Jesus — and only in Jesus! You must rely only and totally upon Jesus for the victory! You must be strong in the power of His Might, not your own might. "Finally, my brethren, be strong in the Lord and in the power of His might. Put on the whole armour of God" *(Ephesians 6:10-11).* To be "strong in the Lord" you must first be "in the Lord" — be "in" fellowship with the Lord. And that means confessing your sins — confess them as soon as they are committed, in order to moment by moment be "in fellowship" with Him — "In the Cross"! Imagine a little door at the foot of the Cross, a room where you can run inside — into the waiting and loving Arms of Jesus — for comfort, for protection, for guidance, for power and strength — "In the Cross". That is how you are "strong in the Lord", by praying and thus bringing all your battles to Him and relying only on Him and the strength that only He can provide to you, to obtain the victory. That "room" inside the Cross is also the "armour room". It is where God equips you with the armour for your battle. That's right, when you are in fellowship with Him, God supplies both the armour and He also supplies you with the strength to put it on. And His armour is not earthly, it is "His" Truth, "His" Righteousness, "His" Gospel of Peace, "His" Faith, "His" Salvation, and "His" Sword of the Spirit which is The Word of God! In other words, He not only supplies it all, what He supplies is "Divine" and therefore "All-Powerful"! And "Divine" and "All-Powerful" is exactly what you want and need when you go into "your" battle! Nothing less will do! Put on "His" Armour! Put it on!

Finally, my brethren, be strong in the Lord, and in the power of His Might.

Put on the whole armour of God, that ye may be able to stand against the wiles of the devil.

For we wrestle not against flesh and blood, but against principalities, against powers, against the rulers of the darkness of this world, against spiritual wickedness in high places.

Wherefore take unto you the whole armour of God, that ye may be able to withstand in the evil day and having done all, to stand!

Stand therefore, having your loins girt about with Truth, and having on the breastplate of Righteousness:

And your feet shod with the preparation of the Gospel of Peace;

Above all taking the shield of Faith, wherewith ye shall be able to quench all the fiery darts of the wicked.

And take the helmet of Salvation, and the sword of the Spirit, which is the Word of God:

Praying always with all prayer and supplication in the Spirit" **(Ephesians 6:10-18).**

In Jesus, In the Cross, is your only hope for victory! The answers lie at Via Dolorosa (*The Way of the Cross*)!

God Bless you in your journey to victory, and God Speed!

Go now! Jesus is calling you! Go right now and pick up your Bible and start reading!

A Closing Thought

Well, there you have it. As you can see, there is much to be said on this subject, but I feel that I covered the most important and necessary bases. So where to go from here? Well, there's one important point that will make the difference between success or failure, victory or defeat. Simply put, it's "Priorities". My friend, what are your priorities? You see, with anything in life we can know the correct answers to the test, but applying them is a different story. Sometimes our priorities can be corrupted, unbeknownst to us. Take, for example, this simple life experience. I'm sure to get a lot of flack on this one, but here goes. Take your average American "Christian" family: good people, hard-working people, and when it comes to their children, nothing is too good, and surely nothing will stand in the way of what's best for them. Case in point, sports: little league, soccer, football, hockey, etc. You get the picture. We, as parents, have been told that sports are good for our kids: they build teamwork, self confidence, self control, etc. Sounds great, but there's one catch. A lot of these practices and game meets are held on Sundays. Interesting...I wonder how that happened? Well that's another story. But getting back to the point, what is a parent to do? Well apparently the answer is simple from what I've observed over the years. Simply put, the sports win, hands down. Why is that? Well, we as parents of young children have been sold a bill of goods. "They" say your kids must participate in sports to be anything in this world: "they simply can't survive without it". Is it really that important? How many really go on to a full-time career as an athlete? Not many. In fact, in time, most will fall away, and by the time they are in their "twenties" and "thirties", they never play the game again. So what was the benefit? Oh yes, the team work, sportsmanship, and discipline. I think Sunday School teaches that too. If anything, the children will grow up remembering that Mom and Dad chose sports over God, so why should I choose any differently. You see, even with the facts in their faces, most parents would run me out on a rail to even question their priorities. They would strongly proclaim that they are doing it for the benefit of the children. To end this simply, we just have to read the Word. The Bible says in I Timothy 4:8 *"For bodily exercise profiteth little: but Godliness is profitable unto all things, having promise of the life that now is, and of that which is to come."* That body exercise that your children will get from sports will only benefit them for a while, but Godliness endures for eternity. And what will "really" benefit your children in their life decisions ahead? You know what's right, but what will you choose? Deep down you may be rationalizing, "Besides, watching the game is probably more fun than church anyway". Just as our priorities can control us and down right convince us that we are right in our actions and motivations, they can also control us in bigger things. "I like lusting after girls" you might proclaim. "I like to look, and when you come right down to it, I really don't want to stop. It's really not that bad is it?" Simply my friend, if you like it, you won't stop it. Do you really want to live a life approved unto God or not? Is your priority in life to please God and grow closer to Him, or is it doing what feels good? If you live by the sword, then you'll die by the sword. We must all ask ourselves, if victory is to be ever attained, "What, and who is my priority in life?" You, and only you, can decide.

Notes

About the Author

Scott Kraniak's deep love and devotion to the Lord shines through! The Lord has used him to bless so many of us through his writings, his sermons, and by his example. He loves and is devoted to his family: wife Julie, and 2 boys, Jacob and Aaron. He and his wife lovingly homeschool their boys. He is a deacon in a small country church. He holds an Associate and Bachelors degree in Theology from the Christian Bible College of North Carolina. He is presently at work on his Masters in Christian Counseling. His future plans include, as God wills and leads, a Christian Counseling ministry to help his fellow believers realize full joy in the Lord, and also to author more books to the glory of the Lord and furtherance of the Gospel of Christ!

Other books...Christian, Children: "Richard Super and his Wonder Chair" copyright 1999.